We hope this little book will
help to pass
until you can once again be
back dancing with us.

    Barbara & Diane Crockett
and all your classmates

THE BALLET

THE BALLET

BY
HUGH FISHER

THOMAS Y. CROWELL COMPANY
NEW YORK

For
PETER
ANDREW
and
JEREMY

Printed in Great Britain

Contents

Illustrations

Preface

"MY daughter, or my son, wants to learn ballet dancing. Please send me a book about it." Mr. Cyril Beaumont, who has a little shop in Charing Cross Road, London, which is famous throughout the world because it sells only books about ballet, the theatre, and the arts, receives many letters like this. Besides being a bookseller, Mr. Beaumont is a most distinguished critic, and the author of many books on ballet, and the friend to whom everyone in ballet turns for advice.

How can he reply to these letters ? He can only say that dancing cannot be learned from a book, valuable as books can be to help teachers, students, and people interested in ballet. Ballet is a living art, it must be learned from a teacher, who in turn has learned from another teacher, and so on back through the centuries. But one can learn a great deal *about* ballet from books and that is the purpose of this book: to introduce you to ballet.

The best way to learn about ballet is to see ballet as often as possible. Every performance will teach you something you did not know before, and will pose questions that you cannot answer immediately. Why, for instance, are two performances of *Les Sylphides* never quite the same ? Why was *La Boutique Fantasque* even more exciting and amusing the second time you saw it ? You compare the castes—were the same dancers dancing the parts ? You notice the programme says : Choreography by Leonide Massine: what exactly is choreography, who is Massine ? Perhaps you will find the answers in this book, and if not in this book in one of the others mentioned on page 93. It would take a very long book to tell you everything about ballet. Mr. Cyril Beaumont's *Complete Book of Ballets* has over 900 pages, and that is only about the ballets themselves, and there is a supplement of several hundred pages, and another one is in preparation. All I can do is to provide a few signposts, and to give the answers to some of your questions.

Acknowledgments

EVERY writer on ballet today owes an immense debt to Mr. Cyril Beaumont, whose encyclopaedic works in particular must be consulted at every turn, and to Mr. Arnold L. Haskell, whose many works on the appreciation of ballet are indispensable. Grateful acknowledgment is made to the photographers whose work is reproduced in this book. My special thanks are due to Roger Wood for so generously permitting me to use so many of his superb photographs.

H. F.

An action photograph by Roger Wood

The dancers move almost as in a dream

CHAPTER ONE

Overture and Introduction

THE lights in the theatre grow dim, the musicians in the orchestra sit quietly waiting. The audience, which a moment ago has been filling the theatre with conversation, is suddenly hushed. The conductor takes his place, he taps sharply with his baton, and in a second the orchestra is ready. They begin to play a slow melody, sad but lovely, the music flows on, and then for a moment there is silence. The music begins again, the great curtain of the theatre slowly rises.

The stage is almost dark, but in the dim moonlight we can see a group of trees, perhaps a ruined castle, and in the centre of the scene are the dancers. Dressed in white, in the traditional

9

They move with grace and precision, weaving intricate patterns

ballet dress, which has been worn since the time of Taglioni, the *corps de ballet*, are grouped round the four principal dancers three girls and one man, who will later dance the solos and the *pas de deux*. The music plays on, the dancers break away, and sweep into the dance. They move with grace and precision, weaving intricate patterns, and when they stand in lines, their arms move together as one, like gentle waves breaking on the shore.

The ballet has no story to tell, but it interprets the mood of the music so perfectly, that always when one hears it again one remembers this ballet.

The dancers move almost as in a dream, recapturing the beauty and the haunting melodies of Chopin's music. The *corps de ballet* recline at the sides of the stage and the principal dancers dance in turn. The male dancer partners one of the principal dancers : he lifts her high in the air, without effort it seems, until she seems to float above the stage. He dances alone, sometimes springing high into the air, but always keeping in perfect time with the music.

The mood of the music changes, and to the lilting rhythm of a waltz all the dancers sweep on to the stage. The music is gay, and the dancers move swiftly and joyously. With this dance the ballet ends and the curtain falls, rising swiftly for the dancers to take their bow. We see them more clearly now, the sylphs of the dance in their long white skirts with tiny wings attached to the backs of their dresses, looking so much alike and yet not alike.

The lights in the theatre come up and there is time to read the programme : *Les Sylphides*, a ballet in one act. Music : Chopin. Scenery and costumes : after Alexandre Benois. Choreography : Michel Fokine. What is choreography ? There is no time to explain now, we must read about the next ballet. This is *La Boutique Fantasque* (The Fantastic Toyshop). A ballet in one act. Music : Rossini arranged and orchestrated by Respighi. Curtain, settings and costumes by André Derain. Choreography by Leonide Massine. There is a long list of characters : a shopkeeper, his assistant, porters, a thief, an English old maid, an American family, a Russian family, a snob, a Cossack chief and five Cossacks, Dancing Poodles, and many others. Then comes the story of the ballet, but before we have time to read it, the lights go down, and the orchestra begins to play. The music is happy and lively and at once we feel that the ballet will be as gay as the music.

The scene is a toy shop, and when the curtain rises the shop is empty, except for two life-size dolls who are dressed as peasants. An old shopkeeper and his young assistant enter. The young man hurries round, dusting the dolls and the rest of the shop. A street urchin peeps in to steal, the assistant chases him but he escapes through the door, almost colliding with two ladies who are about to enter. The assistant starts the mechanism that works the two large dolls, and they perform just like the mechanical dolls they are supposed to be. More customers enter and two dolls are drawn in on a tray. They perform the Tarantella, an exhilarating dance, but they stop jerkily as their mechanism runs down. Many other dolls are

From an action photograph by Roger Wood

Finally come the Can-Can dancers

brought in : the Queen of Clubs, the Queen of Hearts, the King of Spades and the King of Diamonds. There are a pair of dancing poodles and six Cossacks. Finally come the can-can dancers, the lady dressed in blue and a short white frilly skirt, the man very dapper with a curling moustache, a tight-fitting coat and black velvet trousers. They dance with such abandon and skill that the customers are delighted, and an American buys the male doll for his children, and a Russian merchant decides to buy the lady. The two dolls are placed in large tubular boxes, and the customers promise to collect the dolls the following day.

The shop empties and the shopkeeper and his assistant depart. Suddenly all the dancers come to life, but they are a little sad that the two best dolls have been sold, and will be parted. But for the moment they all celebrate with gaiety and zest their hour of freedom.

Too soon, comes the next day. The families arrive to collect their parcels, but to their horror and the dismay of the assistant the two can-can dancers are not in their boxes. The customers leave in great anger, but as they turn and look through

From an action photograph by Roger Wood

They dance with such abandon and skill that the customers are delighted

the windows of the shop they see to their great surprise, that all the dolls including the can-can dancers have come to life and are dancing in triumph. Even the shopkeeper is happy because he still has his two best dolls.

The ballet is full of comedy and character. The customers are all so different and each doll has a distinctive personality. The ballet moves with such speed, there is so much action and movement that one can see it a score of times and still see something new in it every time.

The programme gives a list of all the characters, and if there is time in the interval to study the names of the dancers, you will be surprised to find that most of the dancers in *Les Sylphides* also danced in *La Boutique Fantasque*. In the short interval they have had to change their costumes, their make-up and their personalities.

It is surprising to find that two of the very graceful sylphs were also the very pert french poodles, and to know that in the next ballet they will be something quite different again. The third and last ballet is *Checkmate*. The programme describes it as being in one scene and a prologue, book and music by

Arthur Bliss, scenery and costumes by E. McKnight Kauffer, choreography by Ninette de Valois.

The music for the ballet begins. It is quite different to *Les Sylphides* and *La Boutique Fantasque*. It has a tragic and dramatic sound and at once we know the mood of the ballet we are to see. The curtain rises : two characters, Love and Death are playing chess. Love moves one of the chessmen and waits while Death considers his move. After careful deliberation he moves his piece. Love rises in dismay : there is no move she can make : it is checkmate.

The curtain behind them rises and we see a vast chessboard spread over the stage. Here is soon unfolded a battle between the forces of the weak Red King and the forces of the powerful Black Queen. One of the red knights falls in love with the arrogant Black Queen and his love is his undoing. Fighting for his king he has the queen at his mercy, he forces her to her knees, and pausing in a moment of indecision, she stabs him to death. The Black Queen has triumphed. She harries the Red King, who is too weak to resist her powerful forces. At the last moment he defies his captors, and then falls dead. It is checkmate.

The curtain falls but rises in a second for the dancers to take their bow. The lights in the auditorium come up slowly and the performance is over.

We have seen a varied programme : *Les Sylphides*, a romantic reverie, *La Boutique Fantasque*, with its comedy and character, *Checkmate*, a dramatic ballet with a tragic ending. To enjoy ballet a knowledge of the art of ballet is not essential, and in describing the three ballets in the programme I have avoided using many technical terms : it is unnecessary to know in precise terms what a *variation* is, before one can enjoy it, nor is it necessary to be able to say exactly what is meant by choreography, or to know what *ports de bras* means.

But to enjoy ballet fully a knowledge of the vocabulary of ballet, the words and terms used in describing it, the steps the dancers use, and the arts that contribute to the art of ballet, can help one to appreciate it more.

This book cannot teach you how to become a ballet dancer, no

Anthony

The Black Queen has triumphed

Anthony

From the ballet *Checkmate*

book could do that, but it will I hope tell you a little of the background to ballet : what ballet is, how a ballet is planned, how dancers are made, how some famous ballets were created, who are some of the outstanding people who have worked for ballet, and so on.

First of all : what is ballet ?

One of the best definitions I know is Arnold Haskell's :

Ballet is a form of theatrical entertainment that tells a story, develops a theme, or suggests an atmosphere through the orchestration of a group of costumed dancers trained according to strict rules and guided in tempo and spirit by the music, against a decorative background ; music, movement, and decoration being parallel in thought.

" H'm," you may say, what does all that mean. Read it again, think of all the ballets you have seen or those I have described. Do they fit into this definition ?

Ballet is a combination of several arts : dancing, music and painting : Dancer, Composer and Painter all play their part, and first of all we will consider the dancer.

CHAPTER TWO

The Dancer

PEOPLE have been dancing almost since the world began. We know from the Old Testament that David danced before the Ark, we know that primitive tribes from earliest times danced : war dances, tribal dances or just for the fun of it. We know that in more civilised countries people danced in the streets and on the village green. Many of the dances still survive today : the Morris Dance, Greensleeves. The most popular survival of traditional dancing is the Square Dance, which has returned to England by way of America. People enjoy square dancing, it has so much more freedom and fun than monotonous fox-trots and one-steps, and dancing has become what it was centuries ago : an occasion for fun and enjoyment.

Dancing began as a means of self-expression, and it was only later that it began to be used to entertain others. As a means of entertainment dancing reaches its highest expression in the ballet. We shall learn in another part of this book how ballet has developed in the last three hundred years, from before the time when the king of France, Louis XIV, founded the L'Academie de la Musique et la Danse in 1661, to the present day. The courtiers of the French court and other courts, and even the king himself took part in the ballets. Today ballet dancers must be most highly trained, and of the thousands of boys and girls who begin to learn ballet very few reach even the *corps de ballet*, and very, very few reach the perfection of Margot Fonteyn, Alicia Markova or Tamara Toumanova, Yvette Chauviré, Nina Vyroubova or Irène Skorik, to mention only six of the outstanding women dancers of today.

Why is this ? Why is it so difficult to become a dancer ? What are the qualities necessary to make a perfect dancer ?

Anthony

MARGOT FONTEYN as Aurora in
The Sleeping Beauty

They are : physique, beauty, technique, musicality, intelligence, personality and a power to project.   I will explain what is meant by all these things :

First of all *physique*.   The dancer is like an instrument in an orchestra : a violin, a 'cello or a piano.   All musicians strive to possess the finest instrument they can.   They know that all their years of training and study will be better displayed if they have a perfect instrument to perform upon.   The dancer's instrument is her body : from the top of her head to the tips of her toes.   The great dancer must be born with a perfect instrument, and it must be trained and developed when the time comes.   It is not easy to tell, even when a child is ten or eleven years old, how her body will develop.   Many children who begin serious training for ballet at Sadler's Wells School and other schools have to fall

An action photograph by Roger Wood
ALICIA MARKOVA in
Casse Noisette

out on the way. They grow too tall, or their legs or feet show that they can never become ever moderately good dancers.

Beauty: Physical beauty is desirable, but not necessarily the kind of beauty that film stars possess: it is much more than that. The dancer must be able to convince the audience that she is beautiful; she must be able to express beauty not only in her face but in her whole body. Some famous dancers do not possess off the stage, what is usually called 'a beautiful face,' but on the stage they can convince us that they are indeed beautiful. With their training in dancing and stagecraft allied to natural grace they can convey true beauty and convince us all.

Technique : Some people have a very pleasant and natural singing voice and they give pleasure to their families and friends. But they can never become really first-class singers without learning a great deal about the technique of singing, breath control, voice production and so on. And so it is with a musician, a painter or a composer : they must learn the technique of their art before they can begin to express fully their natural gifts for it. It is the same with the dancer. But technique in all the arts is only a means to an end. It is the means by which a dancer can convey every emotion required of her, perform every step that the dance demands. Technique must never be obvious. Some dancers almost seem to say : " Look, this is going to be difficult." They have an air of concentration and determination, and at the

Maurice Seymour

TAMARA TOUMANOVA

end of the dance, they almost pause, as if to say, "There, I managed that all right, didn't I?"   But watch any great dancer, Fonteyn, Markova, Pamela May, Maria Tallchief, Beryl Grey, Toumanova, Moira Shearer, and you will not be conscious of their technique.   They use it as a means to an end, and it is only part of the means by which they achieve an outstanding performance.

Technique can be acquired by most dancers providing their

training starts early and before their limbs become too set.
But there are some things that cannot be taught : ease of
movement and grace are essentially natural qualities. But although they cannot be taught, training can improve whatever is
there. Beryl Grey, for instance, is unusually tall for a dancer,
and her arms especially might have prevented her advance as a
dancer. But with training she has learned to use her arms so well
that the beauty of her performance is enhanced. Training,
as in Beryl Grey's case, should always develop whatever natural
qualities a dancer may possess. These qualities and the physique
of a dancer must be studied carefully by her teachers and developed accordingly. A few dancers can dance almost any type
of part, others have a natural aptitude for character or comedy
rôles, and the good teacher will see this from an early stage, and
train her pupil accordingly.

Musicality : Music is essential to ballet. Some dancers have
doubted this and have tried to dance without music, and without any great success. Serge Lifar and David Lichine, both
distinguished dancers in the Russian tradition, have created
ballets either without music or with simple rhythmic accompaniment. Interesting as these ballets were, they were only
experiments and the only thing they proved was that music is an
essential part of the art of ballet.

The dancer must possess a sense of rhythm, and much more
than that. She must be able to interpret the music to the
audience. In *Les Sylphides* as we have seen, there is no story to
tell, it is only the mood and feeling of the music that the dancer
has to convey. She cannot do this if all she does is to keep to the
rhythm of the music. She must feel it and understand it, and
in this way convey to the audience its true meaning. She must
learn all she can about music, and the more she learns, the more
she will respect it. Music must not be tampered with, cutting a
few bars here and a few bars there, to satisfy a dancer's vanity.
The music is as important in its way as the dancer.

Intelligence : A dancer must use her mind as well as her body.
The Imperial Russian School of Ballet recognised this, and in one
of the best books on the ballet ever written, *Theatre Street* by
the great Russian dancer Tamara Karsavina, we can read how the

Walter E. Owen   Lido

MARIA TALLCHIEF   ROLAND PETIT

dancers of the Russian ballet were trained both in mind and in body. It is not only physical training that will produce a dancer. A General Certificate of Education or its equivalent is the minimum standard that a dancer should achieve while she is still training. Too often in the past students at ballet schools have not even reached this standard of education. The dancer must study not only music but other arts and subjects as well; painting, sculpture, the theatre, costume, the history of ballet. She must be able to discuss, not only ballet in its widest sense, but the other arts that comprise it. Acting, and especially mime, form an important part of a dancer's training, and the students at all good ballet schools are encouraged to see plays, to go to concerts, to visit art galleries, and to use the library to learn more about the arts and to increase their general knowledge. For too long in England, America and elsewhere a dancer's general education has been neglected. There are indeed, hundreds of little ballet schools and dancing academies, where the teachers think that all they have to do is to turn out boys and girls who can perform a few steps and dances. The Royal Academy of Dancing has recognised the one-sidedness of much of the training given in former years, and is doing its best to establish a higher standard of cultural education among its teachers who teach the many thousands of students taking the R.A.D. examinations every year.

When a dancer is studying a rôle, learning the dances is not the most difficult part of it. She has to create a character, evoke an atmosphere, a mood, and with a thousand touches suggest that she is living the part physically and emotionally. When she realises fully how much she has to learn before she can give a performance that will rank with any of the ballerinas of the past then she is on her way to being a ballerina herself.

Projection : There is one other quality that the dancer must possess, and that is *projection :* an ability to communicate her emotions and feelings to an audience—to " put it over." The personality of any dancer depends partly upon the qualities she has inherited, partly upon the way in which these natural qualities have been trained and developed. Experience added to these may help to produce the kind of personal magnetism that is conveyed to an audience the moment a dancer or an actor comes on to the stage, warming and stimulating them.

The young Fonteyn of 1936 was like a flower in bud, full of promise, with a beauty that was still immature, and sharing with her audience only a little of the emotion she felt. She was then an artist in the making. Her technique developed, her emotional range expanded, her power of projection increased, until it seemed that she had reached perfection.

Then in 1949 the Sadler's Wells Ballet went to America, and when they returned we saw a new and even greater Fonteyn. She had a new assurance, a new beauty, she commanded the stage and she conquered anew an audience who had already hailed her as the first English-produced ballerina. I remember especially a performance of *Swan Lake* in 1950, when she reached new heights in the portrayal of the role of Odette-Odile, and even the critics, some of whose memories go back to the great ballerinas of other times, Karsavina, Pavlova and others applauded her as enthusiastically as the youngest balletomane, but

The young Fonteyn—
A flower in bud, full
of promise.

Anthony

not perhaps for the same reason. The younger members of the audience feel only the impact of the moment, the critics have a standard of measurement that compares her achievement with the great ones of the past. Have I made clear this point about *projection*, this getting across to an audience? It is more than " star quality." Sometimes, in a play, it is a small part actor who gains your attention, and has this magic magnetic quality.

If you have seen *The Sleeping Beauty* with Fonteyn dancing the Princess Aurora and on another day you have seen the newest Aurora, Rosemary Lindsay, you will see what I mean. Rosemary Lindsay is full of promise, she has a spark that one day may set the theatre alight with enthusiasm, but not yet.

Miss Fonteyn, Miss Lindsay, every ballerina, every dancer, does not rest on her laurels. They continue to learn more about their art, they go to classes daily, and when opportunity offers, to the great teachers of dancing.

CHAPTER THREE

The Choreographer

THE choreographer is a designer of ballet. This brief
definition describes what his function is. He arranges the
dances : it can be stated as simply as that. He is like a
dramatist who writes a play, and he is also like a producer who
transfers to the stage the author's intentions. He is both author
and producer. He is like a composer orchestrating a piece of
music, and the dancers are his instruments. He creates that
part of the ballet which is danced, and always he must work in
close collaboration with the other elements in ballet : the
dancers, the music, the scenery and costumes, and the people
responsible for them, and the dancers. It is a task requiring
exceptional qualifications. The choreographer must understand
the technique of ballet, and without exception choreographers
have always been dancers. In no other way can he understand the powers and limitations of the dancer. He must have
a practical knowledge and understanding of music, and a
knowledge of the visual arts, painting and sculpture. And
above all he must have the desire for self-expression, for creation,
and the ability to pass on this urge to the dancers. He can only
do this if he understands people : the way they think, and
the way they behave in all kinds of situations. This long list
of qualifications explains why there have been and why there are
so few great choreographers. It is only in the last fifty years
that ballet has been re-born and many great works created, and
in this time there have been only a handful of great choreographers : Michel Fokine, Leonide Massine, Georges Balanchine, Bronislava Nijinska, all dancers of the Russian tradition,
Ninette de Valois, Frederick Ashton, Anthony Tudor in English
ballet, and in the U.S.A. Jerome Robbins and Agnes de Mille in a

25

Ballet for Boys and Girls

A Balanchine ballet: *Symphonie Concertante*

limited category of ballets. Robert Helpmann has created five ballets, but with the exception of *Hamlet*, they depend too much upon his own personality to survive. Andrée Howard and John Cranko are today fulfilling their early promise, and in time may be added to the short list of great choreographers. Roland Petit, a young Frenchman has had great success and great failure, and whether any of his ballets will survive without the dancers for whom they were created is doubtful. One of his earlier works, *Les Forains*, which shows a group of travelling entertainers, has been revived recently, and although this production no longer has the magic and pathos it had originally, it can still move and delight, even though indifferently performed, a sign that perhaps Petit's talents will one day produce works of lasting worth.

Serge Lifar, a protégé of Serge Diaghileff, a dancer of outstanding merit and exceptional intelligence, has produced many works, some experimental, some in the great tradition of romantic ballet. As maître de ballet at the Paris Opéra he is in the fortunate position of having a company at his command, but of his many works few have survived more than a season or two. Perhaps one of his latest works *Blanche-Neige*, the tale of Snow-white and the Seven Dwarfs, may achieve a permanent place in the repertoire.

Most people it is said, can write one novel, and possibly most dancers could produce one ballet, but whether their ballets will live is extremely uncertain. Michael Somes, the premier danseur of The Sadler's Wells Ballet, has produced for the second company, the Sadler's Well Theatre Ballet, *Summer Interlude*, an unpretentious work with considerable charm ; which makes one hope he will produce other works. David Paltenghi, another dancer, has created several small-scale works for the Ballet Rambert, and Walter Gore and Frank Staff have also produced many works suited to the abilities of the dancers in this small but important company.

Choreography cannot be taught, it can only be learned by experience, by trial and error, and then only by the few who are born with the right creative instinct. The cost of producing a new ballet is considerable and no company, even those with the financial backing of the State such as the Paris Opéra and the Sadler's Wells Ballet, can afford to experiment and entrust the creation of new ballets to new and untried choreographers. In England we are fortunate in having such an organisation as the Ballet Workshop, whose primary aim is to give opportunities, on a limited scale it is true and on a stage like a pocket handkerchief, to would-be choreographers. Ballet Workshop gives regular Sunday evening performances at the Mercury Theatre in London, the home of the Ballet Rambert, and although their first few seasons have produced no new choreographer of outstanding merit, it is doing valuable pioneer work.

Sadler's Wells Theatre Ballet has been in a position to do more for new choreographers, and many of the ballets created specially for this young company have been by choreographers who have not had previously much opportunity or experience in creating new works. John Cranko, with *Beauty and the Beast*, *Pineapple Poll* and *Harlequin in April* has won his spurs as a

A Fokine Ballet:
Dances from Prince Igor.
A revival by Festival Ballet with
Paula Hinton, Vassilie Trunoff
and Daphne Dale

Paul Wilson

choreographer. He has recently created a new ballet for the
senior Sadler's Wells Company: *Bonne Bouche.*

Celia Franca, a dancer of great charm and outstanding ability,
is another who has been enabled to produce ballets for the
Theatre Ballet : *Khadra*, a ballet with a setting like a Persian
miniature, is a most successful work and has maintained its
place in the repertoire for several years. Celia Franca has also
worked with success for television, the newest medium for
ballet, and one which has given opportunities to a number of
prentice hands.

There is no routine formula for creating a ballet, any more than
there can be for writing a play or novel : but two famous
choreographers, Noverre in the 18th century, and Fokine in
this century, have laid down certain principles for the guidance
of the choreographer. Some of them have already been
mentioned : a practical knowledge of music, an understanding
of psychology, an awareness of the limitations of ballet : which
situations can be expressed by dancing and which cannot.
Until Fokine's advent as a choreographer, dancing for dancing's
sake had overwhelmed all else in ballet. Ballet as we shall see

in another chapter of this book, was slowly declining at the beginning of this century. Scores of new ballets were produced but they all followed the same pattern. Whatever the setting of the ballet—whether it was Burma, China or Caxton's printing press (Scene I of *The Press*, a ballet in three scenes produced at the Empire Theatre, London in 1898)—the dances were in the classical tradition, and the dancers usually on *pointe* performed the steps in a set order. If a dancer had some speciality, perhaps an ability to perform an astonishing number of *fouettés*, then this feat would be incorporated into every ballet in which she appeared, and the dancer would bow to the applause of the audience before returning to resume her rôle and proceed with the next part of the ballet.

Fokine believed that ballet was not " dancing for dancing's sake." Dancing he insisted, was only part of the whole. The dances must be in harmony with the setting of the ballet, and the music must be in sympathy with its character and mood.

If necessary, Fokine insisted, new forms of movement must be invented. In the *Polovtsian Dances* from *Prince Igor*, he devised dances that fitted exactly the rhythms of the music : first languorous then suddenly fiery and pulsating mounting to a climax in keeping with the excitement of Rimsky Korsakov's music. The steps and movements in this ballet were far removed from the classic ballet, and this innovation was regarded with horror by the pedants of the period.

Dancing should be interpretive, was a rule that Fokine laid down for himself and his successors and it must never degenerate into mere gymnastics. The dancing must show unity of conception, that is dancers must always keep within the framework of the ballet, they must preserve the character of the personality they are dancing. The dancer must be expressive from head to foot, and every movement or gesture must contribute to the action of the ballet. The traditional mime, as used in *Swan Lake* and other classical ballets, should be avoided unless it suits the action of the ballet. And finally, in ballet, dancing must be on equal terms with the music and the décor.

Fokine who died in 1942, himself produced more than sixty ballets. His first ballets were *Nuits d'Egypte* (later re-named

A Fokine ballet: *Le Carnaval.*   A revival by the Sadler's Wells Theatre Ballet

Cleopatra) and *Eunice*, in which he tried to apply the theories he had so carefully worked out. These theories were unpopular with the audiences who were accustomed only to the old stereotyped form of ballet, but as later works followed his theories were accepted and imitated. His ballets all have an intense musicality. He studied most carefully the music to be used, bearing always in mind the theme of the ballet and step by step he would work out the movements and the mood dictated by the story or theme of the ballet, visualising how they would look on the stage with the costumes and the scenery. He began rehearsals with a complete picture in his mind of how the ballet would look in performance. Because of the care with which Fokine prepared his ballets they have an artistic unity and perfection that makes it possible for them to be revived today. Often the revivals are not worthy of the original production but they continue to delight audiences whose recollections of ballet do not extend to the hey-day of Russian ballet in the earlier years of this century. *Les Sylphides* is in almost every ballet company's repertoire, and *Le Carnaval, Prince Igor, L'Oiseau de Feu, Schéhérazade, Le Coq d'Or, Petrouchka,* and many others are frequently revived.

Fokine worked with Diaghileff from 1909 until 1914, and among the last of his productions in this period was *La Légende de Joseph,* in which the title rôle was created by Leonide Massine, a young dancer discovered by Diaghileff. When Fokine left the Company, it was to Massine that many new ballets were entrusted. Diaghileff encouraged the young Massine to study the work of modern painters, and much of his work during the period from 1914 onwards showed the influence of modern art of the time : cubism and later surrealism. But Massine did not allow his work to be over-influenced by the trends of modernism, and works such as *Les Femmes de Bonne Humeur,* and *La Boutique Fantasque* were influenced by much earlier periods, the first ballet by the 18th century and the second by a study of the period of 1865 and the art of Toulouse-Lautrec. These two ballets have characters with an individuality so strong that they are sometimes almost creatures of burlesque. They were the fore-runners of many similar works, *Le Beau Danube,* a light-hearted frolic to Strauss music, *Union Pacific,* a ballet with an American setting, *Gaieté Parisienne,* an amusing comedy ballet to the infectious music of Offenbach, *Mam'zelle Angot,* a ballet re-created for Sadler's Wells Ballet with enchanting sets by André Derain and music by Lecocq.

Among the ballets in which Massine collaborated with artists associated with modern trends in art must be mentioned *Parade* (1917) for which Jean Cocteau wrote the book and Pablo Picasso designed the scenery and costumes, *Le Tricorne,* with music by Manuel de Falla and scenery and costumes by Picasso, and *Jeux D'Enfants* to the music of Bizet and with costumes and scenery by the surrealist artist Miro.

The work of Massine which has aroused most controversy are his " symphonic " ballets. The first of these ballets were : *Les Présages* to Tchaikovsky's Fifth Symphony, and *Choreartium* to Brahms's Fourth Symphony. They have no characters in the accepted sense of the word and no story. They are attempts to show movement parallel in thought to the music. Further mention of this experiment will be made later.

Massine's ballets, it will be realised, are astonishingly varied, but they have one thing in common : there are no passages of mimed action. All actions and gestures are part of the dance. In *Swan Lake*, *Giselle* and the other classic ballets there are many scenes played in mime, when the dancers use a highly artificial and stylised form of gesture to convey essential parts of the story of the ballet. We tolerate mime as an interval between dances, rather than for the enjoyment of it, however well it is done. It is felt by many ballet critics that dancers in England and America have neglected the art of mime, and that if they were more accomplished in the art the mimed passages would be more effective and less irritating than they are so often today.

Massine has no fixed method when preparing a ballet. He does not, he once said, work out beforehand scenes and dances in detail. He has an idea but it is not fully developed until he has the dancers to work upon. He regards them as puppets : he pulls the strings and tells them what to do ; but unlike puppets he expects them to remember what he has taught them. Some of his ballets have taken a very long time to prepare ; others he has thrown off quickly and with too little preparation. His ballets which are likely to live are those having a strong story and with clearly defined characters, *La Boutique Fantasque*, *Le Tricorne*, *Le Beau Danube* and *Les Femmes de Bonne Humeur*.

One reason why many of Massine's ballets will not survive, is that for many years he has not been attached for a lengthy period to any particular company. He joins a company, produces one or two new ballets, supervises the revival of old works, and then departs to join another troupe for a short time. For this reason performances of his ballets are sometimes given which have little relation to the original work. Massine is not there to keep an eye on his work, and with the change of dancers in a company, dances, movements, subtle points of character, are lost. Some maîtres de ballet have exceptional memories. Serge Grigorieff, for instance, who worked for Diaghileff for

A Massine ballet: *Le Beau Danube*.   A production by Ballets de Paris

many years and later for Colonel de Basil, was able to remember, with the help of the dancers, ballets that had not been performed for years.

But many other maîtres de ballet do not possess a memory like Grigorieff's.   It is difficult to record in detail the movements of a modern ballet.   Attempts have been made, with some success, to record the steps and movements of ballets which use only the classical technique, but so far few of the efforts made to record a modern ballet have been successful.   The most obvious method is to make a film of the ballet, but this is a costly matter and few companies have money to spare for such expensive experiments.

The ballets of this century which are likely to live are those in the repertoire of an established company, where the ballets are danced with some frequency and the parts handed on from one dancer to another.   Unfortunately there are few companies in the world, apart from the State subsidised organisations, whose existence has any hope of permanency.   Thus many fine

c

ballets are performed for a season and then lost for ever.   Most of the ballets created by Ninette de Valois and Frederick Ashton have been for the Sadler's Wells Ballet Company, and it is reassuring to know that the ballets which merit survival will be kept in the repertoire, so long as there is a demand for them. There will be many references to Madame de Valois and her many contributions to the ballet scene, elsewhere in this book, but here our concern is with her as choreographer.

Ninette de Valois has a fine musical sense but in most of her ballets it is the strong dramatic action that first compels attention.   She has turned to literature or painting for the inspiration for her finest work.   She was a member of Diaghileff's company and was grounded in the Fokine conception of what a ballet should be.   She danced in ballets by Fokine and Balanchine, and had personal experience of how Massine and Nijinska worked when creating ballets.

Madame de Valois is a methodical worker, and her ballets reflect this.   The characters in them are not created, as are so many ballets, with special dancers in mind, and they do not rely for their effect on one or two spectacular performances.   The small parts as well as the leading rôles all provide opportunities for real and definite characterisation.

Her first great work was *Job*, first performed in 1931.   Inspired by William Blake's designs for *The Book of Job*, she created with the help of Geoffrey Keynes who had made a special study of Blake, a dramatic and exciting work.   It is more a masque for dancing than pure ballet, using movements not generally used in traditional ballet forms, but it has held its place in the repertoire for over twenty years.   The music for it, written by Ralph Vaughan Williams has contributed greatly to its success.   It was the first great English ballet ; the first not only in time, but in mood and feeling.   Diaghilieff, to whom the idea had been first suggested, rejected it as being " too English."   The English tradition in ballet began with this work. Miss de Valois created many ballets for her young company the Vic-Wells Ballet, some of them modest, unpretentious works that employed the growing talents of her young company. Then came *The Haunted Ballroom* in 1934, a ghostly romantic

An action photograph by Roger Wood

A de Valois ballet: *Job*

ballet that still retains its place in the repertoire. Its score by Geoffrey Toye is not outstanding although it contains one melody that has achieved great success and is a popular piece with light orchestras and military bands.

Her next major work was *The Rake's Progress* in 1935. Inspired by the famous series of paintings of the same name by William Hogarth, it shows episodes in the life of a young man in the 18th century, who spends his fortune unwisely, losing all his friends save one in the process, and finally dying in a mad house. The music by Gavin Gordon, the scenery and costumes by Rex Whistler and Miss De Valois's skill in creating character and developing the dramatic tension of her theme, makes it an exciting work, and one that must be counted as a major contribution to our still young National Ballet.

The Gods Go a-Begging produced in 1935 and *Checkmate*, produced in 1937 when the Sadler's Wells Company paid a special visit to Paris, are two other important works. Since 1937 Madame de Valois has produced very few new ballets. Her

An Ashton ballet: *Tiresias.*   The Sadler's Wells Ballet, with Margot Fonteyn

time has been fully occupied in building up the strength of the
Sadler's Wells Company, and in later years the Sadler's Wells
Theatre Ballet, and the ballet school, and numerous other
activities.   Occasionally she finds time to produce a new ballet
and two that must be mentioned are *The Prospect Before Us,*
and *Don Quixote.*

FREDERICK ASHTON

Frederick Ashton's first ballet was produced in 1926.   It was
an item in a revue *Riverside Nights* at the Lyric Theatre,
Hammersmith, and was an amusing trifle called the *Tragedy of
Fashion or The Scarlet Scissors.*   The dancers in it included
Marie Rambert and Ashton himself.   Since that time he has
produced over fifty ballets including two full length works :
Cinderella in 1948 and *Sylvia* in 1952.   He moves from the
comedy of *Les Patineurs* to the tragedy of *Dante Sonata,* from
the froth and burlesque of *Les Sirènes* to the drama of *Tiresias,*

An Ashton ballet: *Cinderella*.   The Sadler's Wells Ballet

and from the fairy tale of *Cinderella* with its charm and magic to
the heat and passion of *Daphnis and Chloe* and the beauty and
perfection of *Symphonic Variations*.   He has a great feeling and
understanding of music, inventive powers that are as fresh today
as ever and a genius for stimulating his dancers and securing
their co-operation.   The range of his work is extraordinary : it
has wit, elegance and beauty, and his sense of good taste rarely
deserts him.   But for all his talents he owes a great debt to
his collaborators : and he would, I think, be the first to admit it,
to Madame Rambert who encouraged him in his youth and for
whom he produced many ballets on the miniature stage at the
Mercury Theatre, and to Madame de Valois and the Sadler's
Wells Company who provided him with a larger stage and a
company that has grown steadily in talent and numbers.

CHAPTER FOUR

The Story

SOME ballets have no story. *Les Sylphides*, *Symphonic Variations*, and many of Balachine's ballets use the music for their theme, evoking its mood and character. Sometimes as with Balanchine, the ballet attempts to show on the stage the pattern of the music. The dancers are like puppets or notes on a piano ; they have no individual character to portray and they are not expected to show any personality. All they are required to do is to dance, but to dance so perfectly that they and the music are one. Some ballets of this type are successful, they have an indefinable atmosphere of perfection, no story is needed, they are complete without it.

At the other extreme are ballets with so much story that lengthy programme notes are needed to tell the audience what it is all about. For instance, in one recent ballet, *Donald of the Burthens*, created for the Sadler's Wells Company by Leonide Massine, Donald, a woodcutter, meets a stranger who says to him, according to the note in the programme, " Donald, I am Death, and if you take service with me, I will make a doctor of you, but on condition that I get you the first time you try to cheat me." A ballet should need no programme note to make its meaning clear, but by what other means could such a statement as this be conveyed to the audience. It is extremely difficult to show Death's pact with Donald in terms of ballet. If it cannot be done then it is clear that the story is not really suited to ballet.

There are limitations to what ballet can do. A ballet must tell its story by means of movement and gesture, and with what help scenery, costumes and lighting can give it. A story for ballet must not be complicated. It can show episodes in the life

An action photograph by Roger Wood

Tricorne.   Leonide Massine in the Sadler's Wells production of his ballet

of a person, as in *Don Quixote*, it can tell a simple story as in *Tricorne* or *La Boutique Fantasque*, it can be a tale of conflict as in *Checkmate*.   It can show passion, love, hate or any other emotion, it can show character, conflicts of personality, and a whole range of mood and feeling.   What it cannot do is to convey to an audience what has happened in the past, or what will happen in the future, it must deal with the present.   It can convey "I love you," but not "I was in love with you years ago," or "I shall fall in love with you one day."   It cannot convey precise and exact information : " I have just passed the General Certificate of Examination, Ordinary Level, and my father has promised to buy me a bicycle," or that rice is 1*s*. 2*d*. a pound.

The first step in composing a ballet is to have a theme or a story.   Sometimes, as in *Les Sylphides*, it is the music which inspires the choreographer.   In ballets with a story, sometimes the choreographer plans his own scenario, basing it often on a legend or tale he has read.   Massine's *La Boutique Fantasque* is taken from an old German ballet, his *Donald of the Burthens* is based on an old Scottish legend.　Sometimes it is the composer of the music who writes the scenario, as in *Checkmate*.　For *The Rake's Progress*, another of Miss de Valois's ballets, Gavin Gordon wrote the music, and the story, basing it on William Hogarth's series of paintings of the same name.　Constant Lambert was responsible for the story and music of several ballets, including *Horoscope* and *Tiresias*.

Sometimes, but not often, it is the designer who suggests the story, as in *Gaieté Parisienne*, for which Comte Etienne de Beaumont concocted a Parisian version of *Le Beau Danube*, and designed the scenery and costumes to accompany the music of Offenbach and the choreography of Leonide Massine.

Giselle, the oldest ballet now performed regularly today, was based on a German legend.　*Lac des Cygnes* (*Swan Lake*) has a book by V. P. Begitchev and Geltser.　It is the most popular of all the classic ballets, which is due not to the story, but to the music of Tchaikovsky, the choreography of Marius Petipa and Lev Ivanov, and the long and arduous part of Odette-Odile, one of the most exacting tests for a ballerina.

An action photograph by Roger Wood

Giselle, Act I.　Alicia Markova and Anton Dolin.
Sadler's Wells Ballet production

An action photograph by Roger Wood

Giselle, Act 2.   Alicia Markova and Anton Dolin.
Festival Ballet production

The classic ballets, *Giselle, Lac des Cygnes, Coppélia, The Sleeping Beauty*, have not survived because of their stories, but because of the superb opportunities they give to the dancer who takes the leading rôle.

Enough has been said to show that the stories of ballets come from many different sources : legends, folk tales, poems and ideas first conceived by the choreographer, the composer or sometimes the designer.   The outstanding fact to be derived from this is that the stories or themes of ballets must be produced by people who understand the medium of ballet : and its limitations : what can be conveyed in terms of ballet and what is impracticable.   It is the function of the choreographer to translate the theme or story into balletic terms.

CHAPTER FIVE

Music

IT is impossible to have ballet without music, although some people such as Serge Lifar and David Lichine, have produced ballets without music of any kind or with only drums or some other instrument beating out the rhythm. Dancing needs an accompaniment, whether it is a primitive dance with the music supplied by voices, tom-toms or the clapping of hands in rhythm. Morris dancing, the oldest form of dancing we have in England today, has a simple accompaniment of pipe and tabor, which stresses the rhythm of the dance.

In ballet the music does much more than emphasise the rhythm : it is an accompaniment to the dancer, evoking atmosphere and mood, it helps the dancer to create the character she is dancing, and it helps her to memorise the movements of the dance. But even before the dancer begins to dance in a ballet, the choreographer must have the music to help him in his task of devising movements to fulfil the requirements of the scenario of the ballet. Which comes first you may ask?—the music, or the story or theme of the ballet?

The choreographer has two alternatives :

    1. planning a ballet to music that already exists.
    2. planning a ballet in collaboration with a composer, who will write music specially for it.

Planning a ballet to music that already exists

Neither alternative can be said to be better than the other. *Les Sylphides* is danced to music by Chopin, which existed long before ; Massine used Tchaikovsky's Fifth Symphony for *Les Présages*, and music by Johann Strauss for *Le Beau Danube*, all of them great ballets in their way. Georges Balanchine has

Frank Sharman

Gaieté Parisienne.   International Ballet's production of Massine's ballet

drawn upon the music of Mozart, Bach, Bizet, Chabrier and
other composers long since dead.

   If choreographers use music that already exists there are two
ways of using it.   Either they use one continuous piece of
music and use it in its entirety, as Frederick Ashton did in
Symphonic Variations for which he chose César Franck's
" Variations Symphoniques for piano and orchestra ", or he can
select a composer among whose works there are compositions
suited in mood and tempo for his purpose, and take short complete items as Fokine did in *Les Sylphides*, or snippets from a
number of pieces, linking them together.   Leonide Massine
has done this with success for a number of his ballets: *Le Beau
Danube* already mentioned, *Gaieté Parisienne* for which Offenbach
works supplied the score, and most famous of all *La Boutique
Fantasque* for which Ottorino Respighi selected and orchestrated
music by Rossini.   In these ballets the music fits the story like
a glove.   It gives the choreographer the greatest possible freedom

in designing his dances and developing the story he wishes to tell.

A ballet by Frederick Ashton, *Les Patineurs*, uses music by Meyerbeer. The music for this ballet was selected and arranged by Constant Lambert, a distinguished composer for ballet in his own right, and from such unlikely sources as " L'Etoile du Nord " and " Le Prophète " he chose music suitable for Ashton's light-hearted work. Ashton's purpose, as the title suggests, was to show people skating on ice. In a series of short dances or divertissements, he shows experienced skaters who move gracefully to the music, and beginners who move with caution and sometimes fall on the ice in a surprised and not altogether dignified fashion. The ballet is full of amusing touches, and with a white icy cloth stretched on the floor of the stage, and the gay wintry scene depicted by the designer William Chappell, the illusion of a winter skating party is complete, even to the snow that gently falls as the curtain comes down. The pompous brassy music of Meyerbeer is exactly right for this amusing ballet, and Meyerbeer is not held in such esteem by music-lovers that they object to the arrangement of his work for a purpose such as this.

Music has been mutilated so often by makers of ballets that with every good reason, music-lovers object when a well-known and much loved work is hacked about to suit a choreographer's or dancer's whim. In the hands of a sensitive musician such as Lambert, the selection can be made and so arranged that it gives no offence.

Three of the ballets I have mentioned—*Gaieté Parisienne*, *Le Beau Danube*, *Les Patineurs* are all ballets of comedy and character, and although they may have a story and occasional moments of seriousness, such as the lovely mazurka in *Le Beau Danube*, it is the choreographer who has called the tune : the composers if they had been alive, might have objected to the use of their music in this way.

When a choreographer chooses one complete piece of music his task is very different. He is compelled by the very nature of the music to plan his ballet to it. He must not tamper with the music, although here it must be noted some choreographers,

VASLAV NIJINSKY in
Le Spectre de la Rose
E. O. *Hoppé*

whose musical sense is not so developed as Massine or Ashton,
have done most alarming things to well-known music, omitting a
few bars or whole passages when it suits their purpose. Fokine's
respect for the music he used has already been noted. When
he used one complete work his aim was to interpret the music,
and the most perfect example of his sympathy and consideration for it, is his ballet *Le Spectre de la Rose* for which he used
Weber's " Invitation to the Dance," and married to it the
theme contained in Gautier's poem, in which the spirit of a rose
given to a young girl, comes to life. A young girl returns from
a ball, and as she rests in her room, she gazes at a rose she has
worn at the ball. She raises it to her lips, to capture for a
moment, it seems, the joy and rapture of the ball, of a partner
she has danced with, of the partner who gave her the rose. She
falls asleep, and the spirit of the rose enters. The spirit dances

and by some magic spell she is drawn from her chair and still sleeping she dances with the spirit, as in a dream. He guides her through the dance, leaping, turning, moving, always with exquisite grace and with joy that knows no bounds. The spirit guides her back to her chair, leans over her for a second, and by his magic she is transformed again into a young girl sleeping peacefully. He leaps away through the window and soon she slowly wakes. " Is it a dream I have had ? " she seems to say. She sees the rose at her feet, she remembers the happiness it has brought her, and with a slow sweet smile she picks it up and presses it to her, as the curtain falls.

It may sound a stupid story, but so might any poem described in a few words. Only the poem itself can communicate its magic. The ballet is, as Mr. Cyril Beaumont has said, " a choreographic poem." The dreamy romantic music of Weber fits so perfectly the beauty of Gautier's poem and the movements Fokine devised for the two dancers.

There are other ballets of Fokine which seem as if the music had been written for them, so perfectly do the movement, character and style of the dances fit the mood and rhythm of the music. *Le Carnaval* to Schumann's " Carnaval Suite," *Schéhérazade* to Rimsky-Korsakov's symphonic poem of the same name, *L'Epreuve d'Amour* to music by Mozart.

Among Frederick Ashton's ballets for which he has used one complete piece of music the most outstanding is *Symphonic Variations* to César Franck's music. It has no story whatsoever, and like *Les Sylphides*, it is pure dancing. There are no characters, only dancers seeking to interpret the music. It is an experiment which is not always successful, but in *Symphic Variations* it is outstandingly successful. Of all the new ballets created in England since the last war, this seems most destined for a permanent place in the ballet repertoire. It has beauty, speed and repose, a rare quality not often found in ballet. It requires six first-class dancers and in the first performance it had them in Fonteyn, Shearer and Pamela May, and Michael Somes, Henry Danton and Brian Shaw.

Massine has attempted a much more ambitious task in his " symphonic " ballets. Here he uses the music of a symphony

An action photograph by G. B. L. Wilson
Les Présages, one of Massine's symphonic ballets

and devises for the dancers steps and movements which seek to parallel the music. Fierce controversy raged when the first of these ballets were created : *Les Présages* to Tchaikovsky's Fifth Symphony, and *Choreartium* to Brahm's Fourth Symphony. Musicians criticized him for daring to use for a ballet music written for concert performance : ballet-goers criticized him for making the dancers attempt to dance music not intended for dancing. In Tchaikovsky's *The Sleeping Beauty,* and in *Swan Lake,* the composer allowed in his music for these ballets, space for the dancers to move into position in preparation for a big movement, and even more important, space for the dancers to break away from their positions after a climax in the dance. In his Fifth Symphony he works up to a magnificent climax, and then without pause the music flows on. In the ballet to this symphony the dancers move into magnificent tableaux, and the picture is completed at the moment the climax in the music is reached. The music flows on, and the dancers hastily break up their tableaux and hurry on to the next movement of their dance to music which bears no relation to their movements.

But the purists apart, the symphonic ballets of Massine are exciting to watch, full of brilliant and ingenious movement, with moments of exquisite beauty that linger in the mind long after the arguments about whether or not he should have used the music have been exhausted.

Ballets for which music has been specially written

To create a good ballet or even a masterpiece, it is not essential as we have seen, for the music for it to be specially written.   And it does not follow that a good ballet with music specially composed for it will be a good ballet : but the chances are that it may.

If the choreographer and the composer work closely together, and both are in sympathy with the work they are creating, it is likely that the ballet will have unity : that the music will help the dancers to dance and to act the characters created for them by the choreographer.

When *Casse Noisette* (*The Nutcracker*) was being planned Tchaikovsky and Marius Petipa, the maître de ballet of the Imperial Russian Ballet at St. Petersburg, conferred together about the ballet.   Petipa handed the composer an outline of the music required, together with the scenario of the ballet.

Here is an extract from the outline for Act I.

1.   Soft music 64 bars.
2.   The tree is lighted.   Sparkling music 8 bars.
3.   The children enter.   Animated and joyous music 24 bars.
4.   Moment of surprise and admiration.   A few bars tremolo
5.   A march.   64 bars.
6.   Entry of the incroyables.   16 bars, rococo, (minuet tempo).
7.   Galop.
8.   Drosselmeyer enters.   Awe-inspiring but comic music. A broad movement 16-24 bars.
       The music slowly changes character—24 bars.   It becomes less serious, lighter, and at last, gay in tone.

It may be argued that by setting a time-table like this is not

The Prospect Before Us. ROBERT HELPMANN as Mr. O'Reilly.
(The Sadler's Wells Ballet)

the best way to secure great music, but no one will dispute the
fact that the music Tchaikovsky wrote for ballet—*The Swan
Lake, The Sleeping Beauty* and *Casse Noisette,* is superb ballet
music. Writing music for films requires a similar time-table.

I once heard John Hollingsworth, now one of the conductors
for the Sadler's Wells Ballet, talking about music for films.
Many distinguished composers have written music specially for
films : Arnold Bax, Arthur Bliss and Vaughan Williams.
Sir Ralph Vaughan Williams, Hollingsworth said, regarded his
work for films as a good discipline : 8 bars for bomber planes
taking off on a raid over enemy territory, 16 bars for their flight,
16 bars for their attack, and so on. Writing music for ballet
requires much the same discipline. It is not suggested that all
composers for a ballet are required to follow such a detailed
schedule as Petipa set for Tchaikovsky, but whatever method is
used close co-operation between the choreographer and com-

D

poser is essential.   Sometimes it is not easy to reach complete agreement ; the first version of de Valois's *Checkmate,* everyone agreed except the composer, was ten minutes too long.   Constant Lambert's last work for ballet was *Tiresias,* for which Ashton did the choreography, and here again, the critics suggested that the ballet was over long, and eventually certain cuts were made.

Which comes first :   the ballet or the music ?

It can be either.   For *Tiresias,* Constant Lambert arranged the story from the many myths about this legendary character and from Lambert's scenario Ashton devised his choreography : in this case it seems the music came first.

Leonide Massine had long wanted to create a ballet with a Scottish setting and having written his scenario for *Donald of the Burthens,* the composer was then commissioned to write the music.   In Diaghileff's day, themes for ballets emerged from the conversations of the little group of artists he had gathered round him.   There is no right or wrong way, providing each artist treats his collaborators' work with respect, and if the music is by a composer no longer living, the responsibility of the choreographer in respecting the music is even greater. The choice of music must always be the choreographer's first consideration, and for this reason he must have a wide knowledge and understanding of it.

Some ballets show every sign of hasty improvisation : the mood of the music is alien to the mood of the story and the décor.   A ballet cannot be thrown together in this way, and unless it is a freak of genius it is doomed to failure.   A ballet must be prepared, stage by stage, and worked out to its last detail by the choreographer, the author of the story, the composer and the designer.   If the composer is dead then the musical director of the company or someone equally qualified should take his place in the discussions.

Mam'zelle Angot. Sadler's Wells production of Massine's ballet
with décor by André Derain

CHAPTER SIX

Scenery and Costumes

THE importance of scenery and costumes in ballet can only
be realised fully when one has seen a ballet performed in
front of curtains with the dancers in practice costume, and
then seen the same ballet with the scenery and the costumes
designed for it. At the first season of the New York City
Ballet in London in 1950, so many of the ballets were performed
without scenery and with the dancers in what would pass for
practice clothes that it was often extremely difficult to remember
afterwards which title had been given to which ballet, and
vice-versa. The choreography of these ballets by Balanchine
was brilliant, the dancing was often superb and the music was
usually magnificent, although not always suitable for dancing,
but the total effect fell far short of what it would have been,
with the dancers in costume and with appropriate scenery.

51

Imagine *La Boutique Fantasque*, *Les Sylphides*, or *Checkmate*, without scenery and costumes. The scenery helps to set the mood of the ballet, the costumes aid the dancer in her interpretation of character. They are indispensable parts of ballet. The same movements look quite different in different costumes. The dancers in *Nocturne* perform many similar movements in *Symphonic Variations*. In the first ballet the girls' dresses are long, with filmy skirts that float as they move. In *Symphonic Variations* the dancers wear tunics that are short, revealing every movement of the body. The costumes for both ballets were designed by Sophie Fedorovich, but so close is her sympathy with the requirements of the choreography that they are as much a part of the ballet as the choreography itself. If we compare the décor of the same two ballets, we shall see again how different they are. Scenery, Arnold Haskell has said, must parallel the music and the movement. They should not obtrude, they should be the perfect setting for the dancers and for the music and for the choreography.

Costumes and scenery are not just an embellishment : they are an essential part of ballet. They should be designed with the same regard for their suitability as the music is chosen and the choreography arranged. Ideally the choreographer, the composer and the designer should work together when the ballet is being planned, and what magnificent results we have seen when this has happened.

So many ballets of today fall short of this ideal. Ballet, as we have seen, is a unity of three artists, the composer, the choreographer and the artist designing the costumes and scenery. It was not always regarded in this way, as we shall see in Chapter 7, and when the art of ballet was reborn in the early years of this century, it was due largely to a man who had no pretensions himself to being a creative artist. This man was Serge Diaghileff. He persuaded artists, some already distinguished in other branches of their art, to design for the stage : notably Natalia Gontcharova, who designed the scenery for *Le Coq d'Or*, Leon Bakst whose scenery for *Schéhérazade* is among the best known of any scenery of the century, Alexandre Benois who designed the scenery and costumes for *Petrouchka*, and Picasso,

Crimella, Milan

Petrouchka, at La Scala Theatre, Milan

whose scenery and costumes for *Le Tricorne* reflect perfectly the
atmosphere of 18th century Spain.   It is difficult to imagine any
of these ballets without their particular scenery and costumes ;
they are an integral part of the whole.

Scenery and costumes have not always been an integral part of
the ballet, they have been an accessory, and the artist has not
been given a fair chance to do his best, since he was not in at
the beginning as he should have been.   Too often, artists unsuited
for designing for ballet have been used.   They have not fully
understood their rôle in the proceedings : sometimes it is found
that the costumes made from their designs are unsuitable for
dancing in.   They may look beautiful when the dancer is static,
but in movement they are cumbersome to wear and lose their
line, and impede the dancer rather than help her.   Sometimes
the scenery is so brilliant it distracts attention from the dancers.

When Diaghileff died and his company disbanded, the importance of décor declined.   In England what ballet companies
there were had barely enough money to pay the dancers.

In recent years however, Sadler's Wells has done much to
restore the place of the artist-designer in ballet.   McKnight
Kauffer's designs for *Checkmate*, André Derain's for *Mamzelle
Angot* (some of the loveliest seen for years), Colquhoun and

Anthony

Dante Sonata, Ashton's ballet with décor by Sophie Fedorovich

MacBryde's for *Donald of the Burthens* and a recent delight, Osbert Lancaster's designs for *Pineapple Poll* and *Bonne Bouche* are a few examples. Then there are Leslie Hurry's sets and costumes for Helpmann's *Hamlet*, strange and surrealist but exactly right for this ballet, John Piper's fine settings for Ashton's *The Quest*, and Edward Burra's for de Valois's *Don Quixote*.

It must be emphasised that it is not only a question of expense which prevents ballet companies from using the best artists available : many of the ballets in the repertoire of Les Ballets des Champs Elyseés were mounted for a song, but they had such distinction and taste that they made us realise anew how important it is to have a man or woman in an executive position in a company who understands what a ballet needs, and insists on getting it. The artistic direction of a company in this respect is too often neglected.

CHAPTER SEVEN

The Roots of Ballet

TO understand ballet today it is important to know something of the history of ballet. Only in this way is it possible to appreciate the value and importance of tradition in ballet. How it is that although ballets themselves are so different they all rest on a common knowledge and use of the technique of ballet dancing. Two of the oldest ballets danced today are *La Sylphide* and *Giselle*. Produced over a hundred years ago they have been handed down from one generation of dancers to another, and in the form we know them today they follow closely the original productions.

Dancing is as old as civilization : ballet is comparatively young, three or four centuries old at the most. The origin of ballet may be traced to the elaborate entertainments given at Court. The masques provided for the entertainment of Queen Elizabeth I and the Stuart kings were elaborate spectacles consisting of drama, music and movement. Often the movements were elaborately contrived with the actors moving in complicated formations, or performing *en masse* the dances of the period. In the courts of other countries similar entertainments were provided. In France and Italy, particularly, the courts vied with each other in providing spectacular entertainments for every kind of celebration, such as the marriages of princes and victories in battle. During the fifteenth century it seems probable that the art of pantomime, which was popular in Roman times, was revived, and stories and legends were mimed, that is, acted without words, while a chorus declaimed or sang the action of the scene. This new type of entertainment is really the beginning of ballet. The earliest one on record was that given in 1489 by Bergonzio di Botta to celebrate the marriage of the Duke of Milan.

At that time skill in dancing was considered an essential part of every courtier's education, and ladies and gentlemen of noble rank took part in these entertainments. Almost a century later, Catherine de Medici, a daughter of Lorenzo, Duke of Urbino, and widow of king Henry II of France, introduced these entertainments to her court. She spent great sums of money on the performances, her object being it is said, to distract the attention of her son, the young king Henry III from affairs of state. The king himself took part in many of the ballets, and his nobles competed with each other in giving similar entertainments. In 1581 Baltasar de Beaujoyeux composed for his royal mistress Catherine, the *Ballet Comique de la Reyne*, the performance lasting five and a half hours. In this work is found for the first time on record dance and music arranged in a coherent dramatic form; that is almost in the form we know it now—a story with action and movement danced to music, but with singing and declamation in addition. The characters, whether male or female, were all played by men and the *corps de ballet* was composed of the ladies of the court. Later French kings, Henry IV, Louis XIII and Louis XIV were all devoted to the ballet and took part themselves in many productions. For Louis XIV, Lully, the court musician, composed more than thirty ballets between 1658 and 1671, singing and dancing both having a place in them. When the king became too fat to dance, ballet became less popular at court, but its future was assured when Louis XIV established in 1661, L'Academie Royale de Musique et de Danse. Eleven years later a school of dancing was added, which survives to this day at the Paris Opéra. Towards the end of the seventeenth century, ballet moved to the stage and was no longer accompanied by speech and song. In 1681 Lully's *Le Triomphe de l'Amour* was performed and for the first time women took part, and no longer provided only the *corps de ballet*. The women were still ladies of the court, and it was not until forty years later, in 1721 with the appearance of La Camargo that the professional dancer took the place of the gifted amateur. To enable her to move more freely La Camargo shortened her costume by a few inches. The audience was scandalized, but by her innovation

Ballet Comique de la Reyne. Beaujoyeux's famous ballet produced in 1581

(*Print from the Raymond Mander and Joe Mitchenson Collection*)

the dance was free to develop and to move away from the slow stately dances of the Court. " By raising her skirt a few inches," it has been said, " she revolutionised the technique of dancing."

The next great figure in the history of ballet, is Jean George Noverre. Born in 1727, he began dancing at an early age, and at sixteen he danced at Fontainebleau. Four years later he composed his first ballet for the Opéra Comique in Paris. He became well known as a dancer and ballet master and his fame spread. He mounted ballets to the music of famous composers of the day, Gluck and Piccini. At the invitation of David Garrick, the famous actor, he came to London in 1755 and stayed for two

years. Garrick described him as " the Shakespeare of the
dance." Soon after his return to France he published *Lettres
sur la Danse et les Ballets*. In this series of letters he lays down
the principles of ballet, and nearly two hundred years later
these principles hold good. He was impelled to write the
letters because of the way in which ballet was being abused.
" People were dancing," he said, " for the sake of dancing, as
it all consists in the action of the legs alone." Technical skill
is not enough. Movement must be allied always to the requirements of a ballet ; it must always express a particular attitude
of mind, and the character the dancer is portraying must be
evident in every move he makes.

In time the principles he laid down were accepted in all the
courts of the Western world where ballet was performed.

Ballet, in its new form, had long been established in the courts
of Italy, Scandinavia, and notably in Russia. Indeed, in 1735,
the Empress Anne of Russia had founded an academy of dancing,
and some forty years later an Imperial Ballet School was established at St. Petersburg.

The technique of dancing developed slowly through the
years. The pirouette, for instance, was first performed, it is
recorded, in Paris in 1766 by Madame Heinel of Stuttgart.
Paris was then, as now, a stronghold of the dance, and it had
a strong influence on the companies at other courts, except in
Italy, which had its own ballet tradition. In Russia, the
influence of Paris was particularly strong, and a succession of
maîtres de ballet had been recruited from the French capital.
One of them, Monsieur Didelot, who arrived at St. Petersburg in
1801, was not content to let his company be a pale imitation of
the Paris Ballet, and he began to develop a Russian Tradition,
encouraging the use in ballets of traditional national dances,
thus widening the range of ballet.

After Noverre, the next great figure in the history of ballet
is Carlo Blasis. In 1820 at the age of seventeen he published
his study on the art of dancing : *Traité Elementaire Theorique
et Practique de l'Art de la Danse*. While paying tribute to
Noverre and the great work he had done for ballet, Blasis
asserted that the technical development of ballet since Noverre's

day had been so great that certain sections of his book were out of date. Accordingly, in his book he propounded his theories on the technique of classical ballet, setting out in great detail how steps should be performed. He recorded, clearly and systematically, all that was known of the technique of ballet. The system of teaching he expounded remains, broadly speaking, the basis of teaching today. He is indeed, as Arnold Haskell has said, " the father of classical ballet technique."

Blasis later founded in Milan, an academy of dancing, where he sought to put into practice the theories he had expounded in his book.

In time this Academy was to rival the school at the Paris Opéra. His method of training and the rules he laid down for the education of the dancer have influenced ever since every enlightened school of ballet. He would not admit pupils into his school until they were eight, nor would he admit them after they were twelve years of age. In the case of boys, fourteen was the latest age for admission. The course of training which lasted up to eight years was carefully mapped out. Blasis's methods of teaching were passed on to later generations. One of his pupils Giovanni Lepri taught Enrico Cecchetti, who became a great dancer, a great mime and, most important of all, a great teacher. He taught Pavlova and other great dancers of Imperialist Russia and the Diaghileff Ballet. His teaching was based on the methods of Carlo Blasis, and has been recorded faithfully by Cyril Beaumont and Stanislas Idzikowski in *A Manual of the Theory and Practice of Classical Theatrical Dancing*, published in 1922.

Carlo Blasis's Treatise was published in 1820, and during the hundred and two years between the publication of these two great books, the basis of classical ballet training has changed hardly at all. Methods of training have been developed more scientifically by Cecchetti and others, but the basis remains the same. Modern ballet dancers must all acquire proficiency in classical technique, it is the basis of all ballet, however much ballets may use other forms of dancing. Classical training produces a perfect instrument capable of all types of dancing, from the classical *Lac des Cygnes* to the bare-footed free movement of *Dante Sonata,* and the acrobatics of *Fancy Free.* There is no short cut to becoming a ballet dancer : the training is long and arduous. It was so in the days of Carlo Blasis and it remains so today.

Two years after Carlo Blasis's book was published a dancer named Marie Taglioni made her debut in Vienna, in a ballet specially created for her by her father, Filippo Taglioni. The ballet was called : *La Reception d'une Jeune Nymphe à la Cour Terpsichore.* At the age of 18 she was already an accomplished dancer, and in reporting her first appearance the press commented upon her grace and promise. Five years later she appeared in Paris, and the beauty and style of her dancing quickly established her in the public eye. She was beautiful and graceful in a way that was new to the ballet public ; indeed a new word, *taglioniser*, was coined to express this new element in dancing. In 1828 she became the ballerina at the Opéra, and soon the public demanded to see her in new ballets with rôles especially created for her. The popular ballets of the time were concerned largely with the gods and goddesses of Greek and Roman mythology, and the heroes and heroines of legend, but with the appearance of Marie Taglioni in *La Sylphide* in 1832, a new era in ballet began.

The scene of *La Sylphide* is set in Scotland : James, a young peasant, dreams of a strange supernatural creature, a sylphide, who visits him, and haunts him when he wakes. It is his wedding day, and his bride, Effie, and the guests arrive for the ceremony. Before the wedding they dance, and among the crowd of people James sees the strange sylphide of his dream, but only he can see her. She tells him of her love for him, how she protects him from all evil and how she brings him sweet dreams. James turns away from her and the marriage ceremony begins. When James takes a ring from his finger to exchange it for the ring that Effie prepares to give him, the sylphide appears and seizes the ring that James holds in his hand. She tries to entice him away, and in despair he follows her. James pursues her, but in vain. She flies away whenever she is in his grasp. An old witch gives him a scarf and tells him that if he entwines the sylphide in the scarf, she will be

MARIE TAGLIONI as
La Sylphide
after a drawing by A. E. Chalon

unable to fly and she will be his forever. The sylphide returns, James enfolds her in his scarf, and clasps her in his arms. Her wings droop and all life leaves her, as she pushes James away, repulsing his love. The old witch laughs, other sylphides come and carry the body of the sylph away. James is broken-hearted. As he moves away from the sad scene he sees his brother leading Effie to church to be married.

The music by Jean Scheitz-hoeffer fitted the story well, but it was the dancing that made it outstanding. Marie Taglioni invested the sylphide with a dreamy poetic grace that seemed unearthly in its beauty. It moved poets to write of her in ecstatic terms. "She reminded me," said Gautier, "of cool and shaded valleys, where a white vision suddenly emerges from the bark of an oak, to greet the eyes of a young, surprised and blushing shepherd; she resembled unmistakably those fairies of Scotland of whom Walter Scott speaks, who roam in the moonlight."

La Sylphide was the first of the great romantic ballets : it opened a new door for the makers of ballets and for the dancers. It attracted poets, musicians and artists to the theatre, and it attracted the public. They flocked to see the dancer of their choice in similar romantic stories : Taglioni in *La Fille du Danube*, Carlotta Grisi in *Giselle ou les Wilis*, and *La Péri*, Fanny Cerrito in *Alma ou la Fille du Feu*, or in *Ondine*, or a score of other ballets.

La Sylphide is rarely performed today, but ballet-goers had an opportunity of seeing it a few years ago when it was presented by a young French company, *Les Ballets des Champs Elysées*.

An action photograph by G. B. L. Wilson

NINA VYROUBOVA as *La Sylphide*, with ROLAND PETIT, in
Les Ballets des Champs Elysée's production

Irène Skorik and Nina Vyroubova both danced Taglioni's role, each suggesting not a little of the poetic feeling and unearthly grace which had moved the critics 120 years ago.

Not many ballets survive for so long as this. *La Sylphide* survives only in occasional performances, and another ballet of the period is really the sole survivor, in that it is danced regularly today, and is in the repertoire of most ballet companies.

Giselle ou les Wilis, to give it its full title, was first performed in Paris in 1841. It is, without doubt, a much greater work than *La Sylphide*. It has the same romantic feeling : Albrecht, a man of noble birth falls in love with a peasant girl, Giselle, and she returns his love. Unknown to her he is already betrothed to the daughter of a prince, and when the lady appears and claims him, Giselle's brain is turned. In her madness she seizes her lover's sword and kills herself. In a later scene Albrecht visits the forest glade where Giselle has been buried. It is haunted by Wilis, strange sylph-like creatures, who have claimed Giselle for their own. Giselle sees Albrecht and is ordered by Myrtha, the Queen of the Wilis, to entice him to his doom. It is a most moving and dramatic ballet, and the title rôle provides a part that demands a dancer who can invest her dancing with all the emotions that the part requires. It is one of the great tests for a dancer, and today the critics still debate as to which ballerina achieves most nearly the perfection in dancing and acting that the role demands : is it Markova, Toumanova, Fonteyn or Chauviré ? The debate will continue as long as *Giselle* is danced, and that is likely to be for a long time.

It is not difficult to see why *Giselle* is the solitary survivor of this period of the romantic ballet. It has a well-developed story, dramatic situations and emotion that rises naturally from them. So many of the ballets provided an outstanding rôle for the ballerina and little else. Ballet was neglected at the expense of the ballerina, and today we remember only the names of the dancers : Taglioni, Grisi, Fanny Elssler, Cerrito. Each had their own following, and people went to see the dancer, not the ballet. The stories of the ballets became increasingly fanciful and absurd, the music was poor in quality, the scenery ornate and lacking in artistry. In Paris, ballet it seemed had forgotten all that Noverre had said. It was the same story in England, and elsewhere, and when the great dancers declined the popularity of ballet waned.

It was in Russia that the first seeds were sown for the revival of ballet. Marius Petipa had been appointed maître de ballet at the St. Petersburg branch of the Imperial Russian Ballet in 1862. Born at Marseilles in 1822, he had grown up in the world of the theatre : his father was a maître de ballet and his mother was an actress. He went to St. Petersburg as premier danseur in 1857, and a year later he presented his first ballet. He was devoted to the classical tradition, the concentration on line, outstanding in the dancers of the French school, but in the ballets he produced he allowed full play to the dancers who had been trained in the Italian school, which developed the technical virtuosity of the dancer.

When Petipa first began to produce ballets it was customary for the choreographer and the scenic designer to work inde-

H. J. Mydtshoy

Giselle at the Royal Theatre, Copenhagen, with Margrethe as Giselle
and Kirsten Ralov as Queen of the Wilis

pendently, and for the composer to be asked for x bars of music
for this or that situation.   When the theme for a ballet had been
decided, the choreographer would work out how many solos,
character dances, ensembles and marches would be required,
remembering the special abilities of the leading dancers at his
disposal. If they excelled at any special type of dance or
variation then, whatever the theme of the ballet, they must
be included somehow in the ballet. The ballets were never
considered as a whole, as an artistic unity. So long as there
was one principal part always danced by the prima ballerina,
the audience was satisfied. It was no wonder that the leading
artists and composers of the day took no interest in ballet.

Petipa was a masterly organiser of ballets, and worked out all
his movements like a series of geometrical examples but he
learned to work in close co-operation with the composer and he
departed from the rigid formula of other choreographers. By
some happy chance, the director of the Imperial State Theatre
commissioned Tchaikovsky to write music for a ballet based
on the story of the Sleeping Beauty : *La Belle au Bois Dormant.*
It was the first time for many years that a composer of such
standing had been persuaded to write for ballet. No one has
ever written more danceable music than Tchaikovsky, and his
eventual success with the music for *The Sleeping Beauty* led
to further commissions, *Lac des Cygnes* and *Casse Noisette.*
These three ballets produced over fifty years ago are in the

repertoires of most of the great ballet companies of the world today, although few companies perform them in their entirety. Sadler's Wells Company is a notable exception. The premier danseur in the company at St. Petersburg when *The Sleeping Beauty* was produced was an Italian, Enrico Cecchetti. Petipa was so impressed by his capabilities as a dancer that in this ballet he introduced a *pas de deux* which gave outstanding scope for a male dancer. For many years the place of the male dancer had been of little importance, but with Cecchetti as the Blue Bird, the male dancer began to come into his own again. In 1896 Cecchetti became maître de ballet, and proved himself to be a teacher of genius.

Among the great dancers taught by Cecchetti were Kchesinska, Trefilova, Preobajenska, Egorova, Karsavina and many others. In turn they have passed on to the next generation of dancers, the lessons they learned from Cecchetti.

In St. Petersburg, Cecchetti laboured until his dancers outshone those of France and Italy. (In England ballet had sunk to be part of a music hall entertainment.) Although Cecchetti had achieved technical perfection in the presentation of Petipa's ballets and the other works in the repertoire, ballet in general had become so artificial in conception and academic in execution that it had ceased to appeal to intelligent men or women. Ballet needed new life, if it was to survive, and most fortunately there emerged two men who were to give it new life and to influence ballet greatly : Michel Fokine and Serge Diaghileff.

E

CHAPTER EIGHT
The Russian Ballet

MICHEL FOKINE was born in 1880 and at the age of seven he was admitted to the Imperial School of Ballet. His progress as a dancer was swift, and it was evident from an early age that he was an exceptionally intelligent child. He was interested not only in ballet but in painting, sculpture, music and acting. In 1898 he was admitted to the ballet company, and immediately he was given important parts in ballets. This was a most unusual procedure as new dancers were expected to dance only in the *corps de ballet*. His progress in the company continued and a few years later he was appointed to teach a junior class. He studied choreography and increased his knowledge of painting and music. In time he found that the tradition of ballet, which sought only to preserve and to prevent any deviation from what had been done before, was becoming distasteful to him. From his studies he knew that an art can only live if it is constantly developing. If everyone who painted had to paint in the same style and manner then in a few years inspiration would be killed and painting would cease to be an art. It is the same with ballet, and Fokine felt that unless ballet developed away from the rigid convention that existed in the Imperial Ballet, it would die. Tradition, he knew, was so firmly embedded in the minds of those in authority, that it was almost impossible to change it. But if he could not change it, then he decided he would leave ballet.

Fokine prepared a statement of his ideas, which have been already mentioned in Chapter III. He believed, also, that full length ballets should be an exception, rather than the rule, and that new life could be given to the art of ballet if short, one-act ballets were produced. He presented his statement together with a scene from a ballet he had written, to the director of the Imperial

Theatres. But little came of it. He was permitted to compose a few simple ballets and a solo dance for Pavlova, *Le Cygne*, which later became known all over the world, but little else.

Then came an invitation which was to change his life, and the life of ballet. Serge Diaghileff invited him to become choreographer of a company he was planning to take to Paris in 1909. Fokine accepted the invitation and was given the freedom, for which he had sought so long, to develop his ideas.

Diaghileff was in his middle thirties when he asked Fokine to join him. Diaghileff was an enthusiast for the arts, and more especially of modern art. With his friend Alexandre Benois, an artist, he had established a journal, *The World of Art*, in which he pleaded that the artist should be free to express his own individuality and that art must be free to develop without regard for tradition. He organised a number of exhibitions to stimulate interest in modern art. At one time he had held a post in the Imperial Theatres but his ideas were considered too advanced and revolutionary, and eventually he was dismissed. His enthusiasm undiminished, but feeling that little progress could be made in Russia in persuading the authorities to admit new ideas, he planned to take Russian art : painting, music and opera, and one day ballet, to the Western world. After incredible difficulties he succeeded in taking a company of dancers to Paris in 1909. Its success was so great that it revolutionised the whole art of ballet outside Russia. Russia remained unaffected by this revolution, and even today it carries on the tradition of Petipa and his forerunners. But in Paris there was no doubt of Diaghileff's success. The critics were astounded by the blaze of colour in the scenery and costumes, in the quality of the music, in the superb excellence of the dancers, and the unity of the whole performance, so different from the productions at the Opéra and elsewhere. The dancers in the first sensational season in Paris included Pavlova, Karsavina and Nijinsky. The artists and musicians that Diaghileff had gathered around him included Alexandre Benois, Larionov, another artist, Stravinsky the composer, Fokine as choreographer, and Cecchetti as maître de ballet. The dancers were all steeped in the classical tradition, but under Fokine's

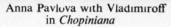

Anna Pavlova with Vladimiroff   Tamara Karsavina as
in *Chopiniana*   *Giselle*

direction they expanded the range of their work, learning to appreciate the ideas and theories that Fokine was now putting into practice, with astonishing success.

Diaghileff brought his company to London in 1911, and it had an instantaneous success. *The Times* praised the technical skill of the dancers ; " Their technique is exquisite ; all of them can do the most wonderful things with no appearance of effort. But . . . it is not in the technical skill of the dancers, but in the variety and imaginative quality of those ideas which the dancing succeeds in expressing that the true difference of the Russian Ballet is to be found."

For over twenty years Diaghileff's company remained in being : the dancers changed, and indeed the dancers who came with him to Paris for the first season were only on vacation from the Imperial Russian Ballet. Although some of them joined him when his company became a permanent organisation, many returned to Russia. In later years dancers who were not of

Russian origin joined the company, giving themselves Russian names. Thus Alice Marks became Alicia Markova, and Edris Stannus became Ninette de Valois. Anna Pavlova stayed with the company for only a short time, and forming her own company danced round the world, taking her dancers to places where ballet had never been danced before. When Pavlova left, Diaghileff had no difficulty in finding other ballerinas for his company : Lydia Lopokova, Lubov Tchernicheva, Lydia Sokolova, Lubov Egorova, Vera Nemchinova, Olga Spessiva and in later years, Alexandra Danilova, were all members of his company at one time or another. The dancing of Vaslav Nijinsky, the leading male dancer of his company, had astounded Paris. They had never seen such male dancing before : his leaps, his elevation, the way in which he seemed to remain suspended in mid-air. When Nijinsky left the company, Diaghileff never found another dancer to take his place, although many brilliant male dancers were members of his company, all of them demonstrating anew that the male dancer is not just a support for the ballerina. Leonide Massine, Adolph Bolm, Leon Woizikovsky, Stanislas Idzikowsky, Serge Lifar and Anton Dolin were among the great male dancers in his company.

When Fokine left Diaghileff, the young dancer Leonide Massine was encouraged by Diaghileff to become choreographer to the company, and among the ballets Massine produced for him were *Tricorne* and *La Boutique Fantasque*. In time Massine left the company and was succeeded as choreographer, in turn, by Bronislava Nijinska, the sister of Nijinsky, Georges Balanchine, and finally by Diaghileff's latest and last discovery, Serge Lifar. Diaghileff was the Russian Ballet and when he died in 1929, the company disbanded and the dancers joined other companies.

" Unique " is a much abused word, but Diaghileff and the Diaghileff Company were unique in the correct meaning of the word. There has never been anyone like Diaghileff. He never wrote the story of a ballet, he was not a dancer, he neither painted nor composed. He was the inspiration of all the artists he gathered around him, enthusing them with his enthusiasms, controlling them, directing them. His company produced ballets so perfect in every way, that the whole course

LEONIDE MASSINE in Sadler's Wells Ballet's production of *Le Tricorne*

of the history of ballet was changed. The ballets set a standard of excellence that is reached only on rare occasions today. What Diaghileff's dancers and ballets were like, how the ballets were produced and the effect upon the ballet-goers of the time is well told in Cyril Beaumont's most enjoyable book: *The Diaghileff Ballet in London.*

In England the influence of Diaghileff in artistic circles was enormous. The young poets, musicians, writers, and artists of the period, Constant Lambert, the Sitwells, William Walton, Laura Knight, Lord Berners, Arnold Haskell, Cecil Beaton, and others, as their memoirs recall were stimulated and excited, and when English ballet was in its infancy many of them rallied round the two women who between them have done so much to create English Ballet : Marie Rambert and Ninette de Valois.

But to return to the Russian Ballet. On Diaghileff's death the company broke up : Serge Lifar went to the Paris Opéra, as choreographer and premier danseur, others went into the commercial theatre, Ninette de Valois a few years later founded the Vic-Wells Ballet. Balanchine and Grigorieff, who had been stage director for Diaghileff for many years, joined Colonel de Basil when he founded his company in 1932.

Colonel de Basil was a Russian officer. He drifted into the theatre when he emigrated from Russia after the Revolution, and eventually became director of a Russian opera company, which gave some performances in London in 1931. Becoming convinced that there was still a public for ballet he set about collecting together a company of dancers, for a season at Monte Carlo in 1932.

The company was formed in association with René Blum, the director of the theatre at Monte Carlo, a man of wide culture with many friends in artistic circles. For his dancers he secured several who had been with Diaghileff, but he had at first no stars : he made them. He searched Paris where famous Russian ballerinas were living in exile, earning a precarious living by teaching. Preobajenska, Kchesinska, Trefilova and other former stars of the Russian ballet had in their studios numerous children, many of them of Russian parentage, and among them were several child prodigies. These children had not had the long, carefully graded education in dancing and the arts, which their teachers had received, but of their brilliance and technical skill there was no doubt. They were really too young and inexperienced to start dancing professionally, but young as they were they had to start earning their livings at the earliest possible moment. Among the dancers selected by de Basil were three children, still in their early teens : Tamara Toumanova, Irina Baronova, and Tatiana Riabouchinska. On these three children de Basil pinned all his hopes.

The novelty of these children performing rôles formerly danced by ballerinas in Diaghileff's Company, attracted the public out of curiosity. They were astonished at the quality of the dancing of these precocious children, and it was soon proved that a public for ballet still remained. In the old days people had gone to see the ballets, now they came to see the child prodigies, and having come, came again.

De Basil had little money, and it was a long and hard struggle

The Three 'Baby' Ballerinas:

(*Top*)
   Tamara Toumanova in
      Aurora's Wedding

(*Middle*)
   Tatiana Riabouchinska in
      Le Coq d'Or
                    (*H. P. Hall*)

(*Bottom*)
   Irina Baronova in *Le Coq d'Or*

to keep the company together. Unlike Diaghileff, he had no wealthy patrons to subsidise his company: either it had to pay its own way or break up. Alexandra Danilova, an experienced and brilliant dancer who had been with Diaghileff, joined the company, Leonide Massine came as choreographer, Serge Grigorieff, Diaghileff's right-hand man for many years, served de Basil in the same way, and he had his three 'baby ballerinas,' as the press insisted on calling them. He had the material for a fine company if only he could keep it together. His greatest achievement perhaps, is that he did keep it together. They lived precariously, they were often hungry, underpaid if paid at all, but under de Basil's courageous leadership, they hung on, and kept together, touring Belgium, Holland, Switzerland and Germany, hoping for success and certainly deserving it.

When the company came to England in 1933 they had almost given up hope. They opened at the Alhambra Theatre in London on 4th July 1933, and their welcome was so great that within a week the future of the company was assured. Toumanova was not in the company at this time, but returned later, and with Baronova and Riabouchinska, the three young girls made ballet more popular in London than it had ever been before. Diaghileff's short seasons had been social events attracting an intelligent, influential but comparatively small and restricted audience. De Basil's Company made ballet popular with the masses. At first his repertoire was small, a few works acquired from the Diaghileff repertoire, and fragments from the classics : an act of *Swan Lake, Aurora's Wedding* (a condensed version of the last act of *The Sleeping Beauty*.) Then Massine began creating new works for the company : *Jeux d'Enfants*, with strange surrealistic scenery by Miro, music by Bizet, and enchanting choreography. It was in a way, a modern version of *La Boutique Fantasque*. Riabouchinska was a wondering child, Baronova was a spinning top, and the ease with which she and the other young dancers in the company performed endless *fouettés* excited an incredulous audience.

The company came to London regularly until the outbreak of the war. It had many troubles, and many of the great names associated with its early years left during the years before 1939. De Basil took his company to America and had his greatest success in the southern continent. Of his baby ballerinas, Toumanova survives triumphantly, moving from company to company as a guest artist. Baronova has retired into private life, Riabouchinska dances as a guest with various companies.

By 1933, English ballet had already begun. Its later success owes much to the interest in ballet created by de Basil and his three baby ballerinas.

CHAPTER NINE

English Ballet

THERE are two great figures in the early history of English Ballet, and both of them are women : Marie Rambert and Ninette de Valois.

The Ballet Rambert

Marie Rambert was invited by Diaghileff to teach his dancers the principles of eurythmics, of which she was an experienced teacher. While working with the company, Marie Rambert became a devoted pupil of Cecchetti and classical ballet dancing. She came to ballet too late in life for her to become a dancer ; she became instead a teacher, setting up her own school, and used Cecchetti's method of training. The Ballet Rambert really began in 1926, although it was not known by this name for some years later. The first ballet was an item in a revue : *Riverside Nights*, presented by Nigel Playfair at the Lyric Theatre, Hammersmith. The ballet was called : *A Tragedy of Fashion or The Scarlet Scissors*. The music for the ballet was by Eugene Goossens, the decor by Sophie Fedorovich, and the choreography by Frederick Ashton, a pupil at the Rambert Ballet School. It was Ashton's first ballet and Madame Fedorovich's first work for ballet.

An action photograph by G. B. L. Wilson

Marie Rambert takes a call

Madame Rambert has a faculty, amounting to genius, for discovering talent, nursing it and bringing it to maturity. Both Ashton and Fedorovich have made major contributions to

English ballet, and it is important to remember that they were given their first chance by Madame Rambert.

Marie Rambert has helped numerous other people to fame, dancers, choreographers and designers. It is both a tragedy and a triumph for her and her company. A tragedy that having nursed talented people, they should afterwards leave her and her tiny theatre for larger companies and larger stages, and a triumph that when one of her protégés leaves she has always been able to find another, and begin her work all over again, nursing, encouraging and stimulating someone whom she believes is capable of developing into a worthwhile dancer, designer or choreographer.

But to return to the history of the company. From time to time her school gave occasional ballet performances, and it was not until 1930 that performances were given more regularly. After a special matinée at the Lyric Theatre, Hammersmith, the Ballet Rambert dancers were invited to give a series of performances at the same theatre. In those performances the great Russian dancer, Tamara Karsavina appeared with the Company, dancing in *Les Sylphides*, *Carnaval*, and in *Le Spectre de la Rose*, in which her partner was a young English dancer, Harold Turner. A famous Russian ballerina dancing with a company of English dancers, was a triumph indeed for Marie Rambert.

If the Company was to develop, occasional performances and short seasons would not ensure permanence or improvement. Soon after the season at the Lyric Theatre and a later season at a more central London theatre, the Ballet Club was formed, and began to give performances on Sunday evenings at a theatre, a parish hall at Notting Hill, which had been skilfully adapted to provide not only a miniature theatre, but a school as well.

The company was full of promising and talented young people, as it has been ever since. Among the dancers in the company in its early years must be mentioned, Pearl Argyle, a dancer of exquisite beauty and grace, Diana Gould, Prudence Hyman, Maude Lloyd, Elisabeth Schooling, and Betty Cuff and Elizabeth Ruxton, who later joined Russian ballet companies, with new names : Vera Nelidova and Lisa Serova, respectively. English dancers always changed their names at this time, not

Les Sylphides. An action
photograph by
G. B. L. Wilson, taken
from the wings, of
Festival Ballet's
production

because it made them better dancers, but because audiences
could not believe that the English could dance.

Of the men who were with Marie Rambert's Company in the
first years, in addition to Ashton and Harold Turner, were
William Chappell, later distinguished both as dancer and designer,
and Anthony Tudor, who has since become famous as a choreographer in England and more particularly in America.

The history of the Ballet Rambert has been told in great detail
by Lionel Bradley, and as a source book it has permanent value.
But for the spirit and atmosphere of the Company and of Marie
Rambert herself, you must read Agnes de Mille's autobiography,
Dance to the Piper. (Incidentally it is one of the few books that
succeeds in describing the trials and tortures that a dancer and
choreographer must endure during the struggle to live and work
in the theatre.)

A year after Anthony Tudor joined the company, his first ballet
Cross-garter'd was presented. He was to present many other
ballets for the company, including *Jardin aux Lilas, Dark Elegies*
and *Gala Performance*, before he left the Company, for New
York where he has since lived. Frank Staff and Hugh Laing

were both members of the Company in the early years, and both have since had notable careers as dancers with other companies.

At the Sunday evening performances at the Mercury Theatre, Alicia Markova frequently appeared, dancing for love and as respite from the commercial engagements in revue and panto-mime, to which she was forced to turn to make a living, when Diaghileff's company disbanded. She danced in *Aurora's Wedding* and *Les Sylphides*, and created rôles in new ballets by Ashton, Tudor and Ninette de Valois.

The stage at the Mercury Theatre is tiny and its stage resources extremely limited. This has meant that choreographers have been forced to create works requiring only a few dancers and comparatively simple staging. Some of these works have been transferred to larger stages with success, notably *Jardin aux Lilas*, which is now in the repertoire of the New York City Ballet, and *Façade*, which both Sadler's Wells Companies have included in their repertoire. But most of the ballets were unsuited to larger stages : they were seen to greater advantage in the intimate surroundings of the Mercury Theatre.

There is space to mention only a few of the other dancers, designers and choreographers who have worked at the Mercury Theatre during the past twenty-five years or so. There is Peggy van Praagh, now assistant director and producer of the Sadler's Wells Theatre Ballet, Rosemary Lindsay, one of the five Auroras in the Sadler's Wells Company, Leo Kersley, Mona Inglesby, who later founded so successfully her own company, *International Ballet*, Celia Franca, who has shown talent as dancer and choreographer, and is now organising a National Ballet Company in Canada, Sally Gilmour, for some years the leading dancer of the company, exceptional as Giselle and in character parts such as *Lady into Fox*. Gerd Larsen, now a première danseuse in the Sadler's Wells Company, Walter Gore, choreographer and dancer, Paula Hinton, and so the list could go on.

The Ballet Rambert has contributed greatly to English ballet. Much of its time today is spent in taking ballet to towns too small to support a full-scale company. But it is a costly undertaking to maintain even a small company, and too often Madame Rambert is forced to economise by having two pianos instead of an

Gala Performance—First produced for the Ballet Rambert

orchestra, by using inadequate scenery, and by using dancers too immature to do justice to the ballets in the company's repertoire. It should be possible to find some way to enable the company to continue its work without the perpetual struggle it has had in recent years to make ends meet. It has done so much, and it has served ballet so well, that its continued existence is most important for the subsequent history of ballet in England.

The Camargo Society

In 1930 the Camargo Society was founded by Arnold Haskell and Philip Richardson, the editor of the *Dancing Times*. Its aim, in Haskell's words, "was to develop and encourage the talent available," and in the few short years of its existence it proved beyond doubt that there was ample talent and that there were British musicians, choreographers, designers and dancers, able to produce new ballets when given the chance to do so.

Several dancers and others who had worked with Diaghileff worked enthusiastically for the new society : including Lydia Lopokova, Constant Lambert and Ninette de Valois. With the co-operation of Madame Rambert's dancers and other dancers available the Camargo Society produced nearly a score of new ballets and versions of *Giselle* and *Lac des Cygnes*. The performances reached a high standard and after a series of special performances which were acknowledged by all to be a great success, it was decided in 1932 to take the Savoy Theatre for a whole month. Spessivtseva, the famous Russian ballerina, danced in *Giselle*, and Markova and Dolin in *Lac des Cygnes*, and ballets by Ashton and de Valois were in the programme. The season at the Savoy was a decided step forward to the creation of an English ballet, and the public began to learn that ballet had not died with Diaghileff and Pavlova. The Camargo Society was doing what it had set out to do. Two choreographers had found immediate recognition, Ninette de Valois and Frederick Ashton, and Constant Lambert had established himself as the musical leader of English ballet. Many young English dancers had proved to the public that it was not essential to have a foreign-sounding name to be a good ballet dancer.

If English ballet was to develop, it must have a distinctive life of its own, it could not hope to succeed by offering to the public a pale imitation of the Russian repertoire. Nor did the Camargo Society ever seek to do so. By its work it made possible the development of an English ballet company, national not only in the sense that most of its dancers were British, but also national in the ballets it created.

The Camargo Society ended its short life with a flourish in 1933 with a gala performance of *Giselle* at Covent Garden. Its repertoire was handed over to the Vic-Wells Ballet, to which we must now turn our attention.

The Vic-Wells Ballet

Since 1914 at the Old Vic Theatre in London, Miss Lilian Baylis had been presenting with growing success and at popular prices, Shakespeare's plays, classical drama and opera. Many famous actors started their careers with her, and a list of those

Ninette de Valois in *A Wedding Bouquet* at the 21st Birthday Performance
of The Sadler's Wells Ballet

who have acted there would include almost every great name in
the English Theatre : Sybil Thorndike, Edith Evans, John
Gielgud, Ralph Richardson, Laurence Olivier, Charles Laughton,
Maurice Evans, Flora Robson, and Peggy Ashcroft, to mention
but a few.

There has never been anyone quite like Miss Baylis. She was a
shrewd business woman with a deep religious faith, and with this
faith combined with titanic purpose and immense determination
she overcame even the biggest mountain. Without any outside financial assistance she built up a National Theatre, she
presented opera, including English opera, and made it pay,
and she founded the Vic-Wells Ballet.

The Old Vic Theatre is south of the river Thames, and Miss
Baylis decided that London north of the river should also have a
popular theatre. With the help of her faithful supporters, the
historical but derelict theatre of Sadler's Wells was bought and

rebuilt. She decided that it would be a good plan to have a small permanent ballet company to provide the dancers for the ballets in such operas as *Carmen* and *Faust*, and immediately set about to form one.

Her rule in life was : if you want anything done, go to the very best people. They will understand, and they will usually do it for far less. For her ballet company she went to the very best person : Ninette de Valois.

Ninette de Valois had danced with the Diaghileff company, and she had later founded a school with the grandiose title of the Academy of Choreographic Art. She had worked at the Abbey Theatre, Dublin and at the experimental Festival Theatre, at Cambridge, and she was closely associated with the Camargo Society.

Ninette de Valois accepted Miss Baylis's invitation. She closed her school, and accompanied by her faithful lieutenant, Ursula Moreton, herself an accomplished dancer, she formed a small company of dancers to dance in the opera ballets.

Greatly daring, Miss Baylis permitted the small company to present a whole evening of ballet. With Anton Dolin as guest artist, this was given at the Old Vic Theatre on 5th May 1931.

The programme was not an ambitious one, but it was in every way an evening of English ballet danced by English dancers. Two further performances were given at the Sadler's Wells Theatre, at which Lydia Lopokova appeared as guest artist. In those early days the dancers included Miss de Valois herself, Leslie French (who was a member of the Shakespeare company), Stanley Judson, Beatrice Appleyard, Freda Bamford, Sheila McCarthy, and Joy Newton.

When the theatres reopened in the autumn, one evening a fortnight was devoted to ballet. In January 1932, Alicia Markova, one of the most promising dancers in the later days of Diaghileff's company, came as a guest artist and the public who remembered her in the Russian company began to attend in large numbers. When it was evident that support would be forthcoming, a special season of ballet was arranged to take place in March, with Markova and Dolin as the special attractions. The repertoire of ballets grew rapidly. *Le Spectre de la Rose*

F

and *Les Sylphides* were revived. *Job* was lent by the Camargo Society, and Anton Dolin gave a magnificent performance in the name-part.

In her excellent book : *Vic-Wells : A Ballet Progress*, Miss P. W. Manchester records that it was not easy to provide Job with seven sons : " They were never the same twice running, and on one occasion they even dwindled to six."   Other ballets in the repertoire were *Fête Polonaise, Regatta*, and Ninette de Valois's ballet to Elgar's Nursery Suite.

It was in 1932 that the Camargo Society gave its memorable season at the Savoy Theatre.   The Vic-Wells dancers and the dancers of Marie Rambert's Ballet Club combined, with other English dancers and guest artists.   The audiences during this season proved beyond doubt that there was a public for English ballet, a small selective public perhaps, but sufficiently enthusiastic to encourage Miss Baylis to plan more ambitiously.

In the autumn of 1932 there were regular performances of the Vic-Wells Ballet with Markova and Dolin as principal dancers. In March 1933, the first full-length ballet was added to the repertoire : *Coppélia* with Lydia Lopokova as an enchanting Swanilda.

There had been little foreign ballet in London since Diaghileff's last season in 1919, and Pavlova's last appearance in 1930, but in 1933, *Les Ballets* 1933, under the direction of Georges Balanchine, and with Tilly Losch and Tamara Toumanova appeared at the Savoy Theatre, and a little later Colonel de Basil's *Ballet Russe* began a season at the Alhambra Theatre which lasted for four months.   With its inheritance of ballets and dancers from Diaghileff's company, its incredible baby ballerinas, the brilliance of its sets and costumes, and Massine with his new ballets, the company had a success which could only be described as sensational.   The Vic-Wells never had a fraction of the publicity or attention from the critics that was given to de Basil's company. But slowly and very surely Miss de Valois was laying the foundations for her company.

Markova was still with the company, and until she left in 1935, she was the great attraction.   She had an immense personal following.   An outstanding event of the season of 1933-34 was

The Haunted Ballroom, in which Robert Helpmann created his first leading role: The Master of Tregennis. Helpmann had made rapid strides in the short time he had been in the company, taking among other important parts Satan in *Job*. It was in this season also that Frederick Ashton came to the company and in December 1933 produced his first ballet for the company *Les Rendezvous*.

An early photograph of Robert Helpmann in *Carnaval*

The great event of the season 1934-35 was the revival of *Lac des Cygnes*, with Markova dancing the dual rôle of Odette-Odile, and with Helpmann partnering her. Among the young dancers who attracted notice during the season for the excellence and promise of their performance were Pamela May, Elizabeth Miller and a little dark-eyed girl in the *corps de ballet*, who earned several opportunities during the season to dance a number of parts, including the solo mazurka in *Les Sylphides*. This small girl, who was at first undecided what name to use, finally decided to call herself Margot Fonteyn. At the end of this season Markova left the company, and shortly afterwards joined forces with Dolin and formed the Markova-Dolin Ballet.

How would the Vic-Wells Company fare without Markova was the question everyone asked with some anxiety ? Would it, could it, possibly survive without a star of her magnitude to draw the public in ? Would it not be possible to engage another great dancer to take her place ?

After the first night of the season in September 1935 it was quickly realised that the company could and would survive without a Markova. The young dancers who previously had been outshone by the brilliance of Markova, matured overnight, or so it seemed, and the company began to show a personality of its own. Some of Markova's roles were taken over by Fonteyn, Elizabeth Miller took over others, Pearl Argyle joined the company from the Ballet Rambert, to dance leading roles.

While Markova was with the Vic-Wells Ballet, Miss de Valois was quietly building up the company, and " in a good company," Mr. Haskell has said, " no dancer is indispensable, that is one of the standards of a good company," and so it proved. Frederick Ashton became a permanent member of the company in 1935 and has been with them ever since. He has produced more than a score of new ballets for the company, specially tailored in many cases for individual dancers.

The company grew in strength and reputation, and in 1937 it visited Paris where the first performance of de Valois' *Checkmate* was given. In 1939 *The Sleeping Princess* was revived and became one of the most successful productions in the repertoire. Year by year the company increased its reputation and its following. Margot Fonteyn and Helpmann were the two principal dancers, supported by numerous other excellent and promising dancers who had grown up in the company since its earliest days.

Then came the war and the plans for the expansion of the ballet school and the formation of a second company and other plans had to be abandoned. The male dancers of the company were called up into the forces, in spite of powerful protests. Bernard Shaw in a letter to *The Daily Telegraph* protested most vehemently, describing the dancers as " irreplacable, rare, highly skilled artists."

Somehow the company carried on. On occasional leave from the R.A.F., Ashton created new ballets for the company. New dancers of talent emerged from the ranks, notably Beryl Grey and Moira Shearer, and a new choreographer was found : Robert Helpmann. In 1942 he produced three ballets : *Comus*, *Hamlet*, and *The Birds*. Later he produced *Miracle in the Gorbals* and the short-lived *Adam Zero*. When the war was over the male dancers returned and soon the company was at full strength again and better than ever.

In little more than fifteen years Miss de Valois had built up a magnificent company of dancers. The classics had their proper and important place in the repertoire but there was in addition a large number of ballets by English choreographers. Miss de Valois was the inspiration and driving force, as indeed she is today.

Maurice Seymour
Beryl Grey in *Swan Lake*

Her most important colleague until his untimely death in 1951 was Constant Lambert, a composer of great promise, and a musician of distinction, with a wide cultural background. He gave the best years of his creative life to work for Vic-Wells Ballet. From its early days Miss de Valois had insisted on the proper importance of music in ballet, and she could not have found a more perfect collaborator. He composed the music for a few ballets including *Horoscope*, and he arranged with skill the music for more than a dozen new works. When the company had to dispense with an orchestra during certain periods of the war years, he rescored the ballet music for two pianos and played one of them himself night after night. For years in indifferent health he laboured on. His last original work was *Tiresias*, with décor by his wife Isabel, and choreography by Ashton. A few days after the first performance of this ballet he died.

There is no space to tell in more detail the subsequent history of the Sadler's Wells Company except to say that the Company now has an international reputation. It has had two spectacularly successful tours in America, has danced on the Continent, and it has filled Covent Garden for months on end. Margot Fonteyn, the first great dancer in the English tradition, is the *prima ballerina* of the company, and she continues to achieve new heights of perfection. With her in the company are no less than five or six other dancers of the *ballerina* class to dance the leading rôles in the classical ballets : Beryl Grey, and until recently Moira Shearer ; Pamela May, a dancer of

Anthony

An informal photograph of
Moira Shearer

great strength, and beautiful line; Violetta Elvin, a Russian dancer of great beauty and distinction; Nadia Nerina, from South Africa, and Rosemary Lindsay. Julia Farron, Gerd Larsen, Margaret Dale, and Pauline Clayden are among the other leading dancers of the company today. The male dancers, with Michael Somes at their head, are stronger in talent and promise than they have ever been. The outstanding male dancers today in the company include John Field, Brian Shaw, Alexis Rassine, John Hart, and Alexander Grant.

International Ballet

After the Sadler's Wells Company, the International Ballet is the best-known company in England and if numbers count for anything, it is probably seen by more people in one year than is the Sadler's Wells Company. Under its founder and director Mona Inglesby, it has taken ballet to towns that had never seen a large-scale company before. It has danced in cinemas and in concert halls, including the Royal Festival Hall, London. It has always concentrated on performing the great classical ballets, *Lac des Cygnes*, *The Sleeping Princess*, *Giselle*, and *Coppélia*. In the production of these it was most fortunate in having the direction of Nicholas Sergeyev, who many years before had recorded these ballets as they were danced at the Maryinsky Theatre in St. Petersburg. It was with Sergeyev's help that Diaghileff had mounted his production of *The Sleeping Princess* in 1921, and in later years Sergeyev performed a similar service for Sadler's Wells. But his greatest work was with International Ballet and when he died in 1951 he entrusted to Mona Inglesby the responsibility of preserving the great classical tradition.

Miss Inglesby dances the leading rôles in most of the ballets in her company, sharing them with a number of guest artists,

Rimis

Mona Inglesby

who have included Nina Tarakanova and Nana Gollner; but in recent years the ballerinas have been recruited from her own company and many of her dancers have matriculated from the school which is run in association with the company. In addition to the classics the Company's repertoire includes Fokine's *Les Sylphides* and *Carnaval*, Andrée Howard's balletic version of *Twelfth Night*, Massine's *Capriccio Espagnol* and *Gaieté Parisienne*, and several ballets by Miss Inglesby, including *Amoras, Planetomania, Endymion*, all of which I hope one day may be revived.

Sadler's Wells Theatre Ballet

Plans for a second company for Sadler's Wells had long been one of Miss de Valois's aims but it was not until 1946 that it came into being as the Sadler's Wells Opera-Ballet. " The formation of this company," Arnold Haskell wrote in *The Ballet Annual*, No. 1, " is important. It provides the machinery for a continuous chain-development : school to second company ; second company to first company. Such machinery does not exist outside state-supported institutions."

An important aim of the company was to give stage experience to young dancers, some of whom would be eventually suitable for the senior company. Another important aim was to give young choreographers a chance.

The dancers in the company were young and comparatively inexperienced. For the first few seasons one or two experienced dancers, including June Brae, Leo Kersley, and Alan Carter, led the company, and there were occasional guest artists from the senior company. From the very first performance of the new company on 8th April 1946 it was evident that the youthful company had already a personality of its own. The ballets for the most part were simple works which did not place too great a strain on immature dancers, although from the start, classical ballet, even if it was only an act from *Casse-Noisette*, and Fokine's ballets *Les Sylphides* and *Carnaval*, were included in the repertoire. The company was under the direction of Ninette de Valois with two able lieutenants : Ursula Moreton, and Peggy Van Praagh who became both *maitresse de ballet* and producer. In six years the company has grown and developed into something more than a stepping stone between school and the first company. While some of its dancers have been transferred to the senior company, including Nadia Nerina, Anne Heaton, and Alexandra Grant, the company has produced its own leading dancers, including Elaine Fifield, David Blair, David Poole, Pirmin Trecu, and others. An experienced young dancer of great promise, Svetlana Beriosova, was with the company as a leading dancer for several seasons but in the summer of 1952 she was transferred to the senior company.

In the Company's short life it has given opportunity to several choreographers: Celia Franca with *Khadra*, and *Bailemos*; Andrée Howard, already a choreographer with an established reputation with the Ballet Rambert and elsewhere, has produced several ballets of distinction, including *Assembly Ball*; Alan Carter, Anthony Burke, Nancy McNaught, and Michael Somes, have tried their prentice hands with varying success. Without such experiments new choreographers will never be found. In John Cranko the Company has discovered a choreographer of outstanding merit and immense promise. He has great musical sensitivity and an ability to create character through the medium of the dance. One evening in 1951 a whole evening was devoted to his works: *Sea Change*, a sombre dramatic ballet to Sibelius's *En Saga*, *Beauty and the Beast*, a simple and refreshing retelling of the fairy tale, *Pastorale*, and *Pineapple Poll*, which from the first performance became an established favourite. As a tribute to the Company, Balanchine and Ashton have both composed new ballets for the Company and Miss de Valois has permitted it to do *The Prospect Before Us* and *The Rake's Progress*.

Sadler's Wells
Theatre Ballet

Ashton's *Valses Nobles
et Sentimentales*

(*Angus McBean*)

Balanchine's
Trumpet Concerto

(*Roger Wood*)

Cranko's
Pineapple Poll

(*An action photograph by
Roger Wood*)

The aim of the Company was to discover new talent. It has achieved its aim in dancers, choreographers, and designers.

Festival Ballet

The Festival Ballet Company was formed in 1950 with Anton Dolin as *premier danseur* and artistic director. Alicia Markova joined the Company when it came to London later in the year. Other dancers in the first London season included Nathalie Krassovska, Anna Cheselka, and John Gilpin, a discovery of Mme. Rambert, in whose company he was first noticed as a dancer of great promise. The *corps de ballet* was largely recruited from a ballet school and, in its early days was obviously young and inexperienced. The repertoire included *Casse-Noisette*, almost in its entirety, Act II of *Swan Lake*, several new ballets which did not make too great demands on the company,

Maurice Seymour

Nathalie Krassovska (now Leslie)
of Festival Ballet

and revivals of *Petrouchka, Les Sylphides, Dances from Prince Igor*, and *Le Beau Danube*. Most wisely, Dolin invited a number of guest artists including Massine, Yvette Chauviré, Tatiana Riabouchinska, Alexandra Danilova, and Mia Slavenska. The company has the distinction of being the first English ballet company to appear at Monte Carlo, traditionally the home of Russian ballet since Diaghileff's day. By this time many of the younger dancers in the company had developed greatly and the company as a whole had matured and was working together extraordinarily well. Today the company is no longer dependent on its two stars ; indeed, Markova has now left the Company, and Dolin dances rarely. The young dancers in the Company, especially Krassovska, Gilpin, Sonia Arova and a brilliant young French dancer, Oleg Briansky, are carrying the burden of the principal rôles, together with Belinda Wright, and other experienced dancers. Nathalie Krassovska is now Natalie Leslie, as it was felt that the Russian sounding name was difficult to pronounce. Gone are the days when every English dancer had to think up a Russian name. Recently the Company has added a revival of *Schéhérazade* to its repertoire, and a new ballet by Frederick Ashton.

The outstanding production that the Company has to offer is *Giselle*. Directed by Dolin, it has a sense of drama and romance lacking in other versions and it has provided two dancers at least in the rôle of Giselle who have brought fresh understanding to this most difficult part : Alicia Markova and Yvette Chauviré.

A Glossary of Technical Terms

LEO KERSLEY, in collaboration with JANET SINCLAIR, has published recently *A Dictionary of Ballet Terms*, with numerous accurate drawings of the steps drawn by Peter Revitt. The length of the book is exactly the same as this: 96 pages. It will be appreciated that the glossary which follows must be brief and necessarily very incomplete. Grateful acknowledgment is made to Mr. Kersley's book for assistance in compiling this glossary.

ARABESQUE.—One leg is extended behind the dancer with straight knee and pointed foot, the supporting leg either bent or straight. The body is held erect. There are several variations of the arabesque.

ATTITUDE.—The pose in which a dancer may finish a pirouette.

DIVERTISSEMENT.—A series of dances, which have no connection with each other.

ELEVATION.—The dancer's ability to jump in the air.

ENCHAÎNEMENT.—A series of steps linked together.

ENTRECHAT.—A jump into the air when the feet change position with regard to one another, four, six, eight or more times.

FOUETTÉ.—A series of turns on the supporting leg propelled by a whipping movement of the other leg. There are many occasions when a dancer is required to perform 32 fouettés, without pause.

MOVEMENTS IN DANCING.—There are seven types: *Plier* (to bend), *Étendre* (to stretch), *Relever* (to raise), *Glisser* (to glide), *Sauter* (to jump), *Elancer* (to dart), *Tourner* (to turn).

PAS.—A step or dance. There are numerous steps, *pas de bourrée*, *pas couru*, etc. When used with French numerals indicates the numbers of people in the dance: *pas de deux*, two; *pas de huit*, eight.

PIROUETTE.—A turn on one leg in which the dancer spins round on one foot. There are a variety of pirouettes.

POINTES.—*Sur les pointes*. On the tips of the toes. The dancer wears special blocked shoes to facilitate dancing on her toes. No child of under ten should be permitted to move on *pointes*, and no one should attempt it except under direction from a professional teacher.

SUITE DE DANSES.—A series of connected dances, in the same mood and style, with music by the same composer—e.g. *Les Sylphides*.

TOUR EN L'AIR.—A complete turn of the body when in the air.

VARIATION.—A solo dance.

A Ballet Library

There are many books on ballet now available. The books listed below are all books which may be recommended for those wishing to build up a reliable and comprehensive ballet library. Many others could be added to the list but these will do to begin with.

Biographical

THEATRE STREET by TAMARA KARSAVINA. An enchanting book in which Madame Karsavina recalls her memories of her life at the Imperial Ballet School in St. Petersburg, and of her career as a dancer. *(Constable.)*

DANCE TO THE PIPER by AGNES DE MILLE. The autobiography of a dancer and choreographer: an exciting and most interesting book. *(Hamish Hamilton.)*

IN HIS TRUE CENTRE by ARNOLD L. HASKELL. Few people have done so much for English ballet as Mr. Haskell. His autobiography has much of special interest to balletomanes. *(A. & C. Black.)*

BALLETOMANIA by ARNOLD L. HASKELL. Part autobiographical, but mostly a critical and absorbing account of ballet from Diaghileff's day, with special attention to de Basil's company and his dancers. *(Gollancz.)*

Reference

COMPLETE BOOK OF BALLETS by CYRIL BEAUMONT. An indispensable reference book containing details of every important ballet in the nineteenth and twentieth centuries. First published in 1937, a supplement covers the four years up to 1941. In time, it is to be hoped, that Mr. Beaumont will publish other volumes of his encyclopaedic work. *(Putnam.)*

BALLET: A Complete Guide to Appreciation; history, aesthetics, ballets, dancers, by ARNOLD L. HASKELL. An admirable and comprehensive book. *(Penguin Books.)*

THE BALLET ANNUAL, edited by ARNOLD L. HASKELL. This record and year book provides a comprehensive account of the ballet year by year. Each issue has over a hundred magnificent photographs. *(A. & C. Black.)*

Appreciation

THE BALLET LOVER'S POCKET BOOK and THE BALLET LOVER'S COMPANION, both by KAY AMBROSE. *(A. & C. Black.)*

NATIONAL BALLET and THE MAKING OF A DANCER, both by ARNOLD L. HASKELL. *(A. & C. Black.)*

APPROACH TO THE BALLET by A. H. FRANKS. A comprehensive and balanced study, with excellent illustrations. *(Pitman.)*

INVITATION TO THE BALLET by NINETTE DE VALOIS.
(John Lane The Bodley Head.)

VIC-WELLS: A Ballet Progress by P. W. MANCHESTER. *(Gollancz.)*

Pictorial

MARGOT FONTEYN, ALICIA MARKOVA, BERYL GREY. Three books by GORDON ANTHONY, each containing numerous photographs by Mr. Anthony, with excellent notes on the rôles portrayed. *(Phoenix House.)*

THE SADLER'S WELLS BALLET: At the Royal Opera House, Covent Garden, by ROGER WOOD. Photographs by Mr. Wood of every dancer in the Company.
(Saturn Press.)

THE SADLER'S WELLS THEATRE BALLET by ROGER WOOD. A delightful souvenir of this young company, showing the dancers on stage and off stage. *(Phoenix House.)*

DANCERS OF TO-DAY: No. 1, MARGOT FONTEYN. No. 2, MOIRA SHEARER. These inexpensive books illustrate fully the most recent rôles danced by the dancers.
(A. & C. Black.)

BARON AT THE BALLET (B. S. NAHUM). A sumptuously illustrated collection of Baron's photographs, with critical notes by Arnold L. Haskell. *(Collins.)*

Ballets to See

If you live in London it is easy to see ballet. The Sadler's Wells Ballet and the Sadler's Wells Theatre Ballet are in residence for most of the year. International Ballet, Festival Ballet and Ballet Rambert have occasional seasons, and there are many visiting companies and dancers from abroad. From the U.S.A. come the New York City Ballet (with its wealth of ballets by Balanchine) and the Ballet Theatre (with an extensive repertoire including several delightful ballets in the American style: *Rodeo, Billy the Kid, Fancy Free,* and the dramatic *Fall River Legend* and *Pillar of Fire*). From France comes the Marquis de Cuevas's Grand Ballet de Monte Carlo (with a repertoire rich in ballets by Massine, Nijinska, Balanchine and Lichine). Indian dancers, Ram Gopal, Uday Shankar and others; Spanish dancers, the virtuoso Antonio and Rosario, Carmen Amaya, José Greco, Pilar Lopez, Teresa and Luisilio, and many other foreign dancers and companies also come to London. There is so much ballet to see in London, it is easy to get indigestion. Outside London, the bigger cities, Edinburgh, Glasgow, Manchester, Birmingham, Liverpool, Leeds and Cardiff have regular visits from such companies as International Ballet and Festival Ballet and occasional visits from Sadler's Wells and the Sadler's Wells Theatre Ballet, and rare visits from foreign companies. Smaller cities and towns are visited by the Ballet Rambert, and the Sadler's Wells Theatre Ballet, and by small companies such as Ambassador Ballet and Continental Ballet.

If you look into television there are many excellent ballet programmes including such semi-technical series as Felicity Gray's *Ballet for Beginners,* and occasionally performances of the full-length classical ballets and individual ballets from the repertoires of the larger companies.

Here is a list of the important works that everyone interested in ballet should try to see. I have omitted ballets which there is little chance of your seeing: Massine's *Les Présages* and *Choreartium* for instance. If a ballet company not mentioned here comes your way, find out what they are doing and do your best to see them. There is always a chance that Roland Petit, or Jean Babilée may form new companies or that de Basil's company will be re-formed. They all have important and interesting ballets in their repertoires.

In the list of ballets given below: S.W.B.=Sadler's Wells Ballet; S.W.T.B.=Sadler's Wells Theatre Ballet; I.B.=International Ballet; F.B.=Festival Ballet; B.R.=Ballet Rambert.

THE CLASSICS

	Created	Composer	Choreographer	Performed by:
1. GISELLE	1841	Adam	Coralli	S.W.B., I.B., F.B., B.R.
2. COPPÉLIA	1870	Delibes	Merante	S.W.B., S.W.T.B., I.B.
3. THE SLEEPING BEAUTY	1890	Tchaikovsky	Petipa	S.W.B., I.B.
4. CASSE NOISETTE	1892	Tchaikovsky	Ivanov	S.W.T.B. (Act II), F.B.
5. THE SWAN LAKE	1895	Tchaikovsky	Petipa and Ivanov	S.W.B., I.B., F.B. (Act II), B.R. (Act II).

BALLETS BY MICHEL FOKINE

	Created	Music	Designer	Performed by:
6. LES SYLPHIDES	1908 (as Chopiniana)	Chopin	after Alexandre Benois	Almost every company.
7. LE CARNAVAL	1910	Schumann	after Léon Bakst	S.W.T.B. and occasionally by S.W.B. and I.B.
8. DANCES FROM PRINCE IGOR	1909	Borodine	after Roehrich	I.B. and F.B.
9. SCHÉHÉRAZADE	1910	Rimsky-Korsakov	Léon Bakst	F.B.
10. LE SPECTRE DE LA ROSE	1911	Weber	after Léon Bakst	F.B.
11. PETROUCHKA	1911	Stravinsky	Alexandre Benois	F.B.

(There are many other Fokine ballets worthy of revival and possibly Festival Ballet another company may add them to their repertoires at some future date.)

BALLETS BY LEONIDE MASSINE

		Created	Music	Designer	Performed by:
12.	La Boutique Fantasque	1919	Rossini-Respighi	André Derain	S.W.B.
13.	Le Tricorne (The Three-Cornered Hat)	1919	de Falla	Picasso	S.W.B.
14.	Le Beau Danube	1933	Strauss	Polunin after Guys, and Beaumont	F.B.
15.	Gaîeté Parisienne	1938	Offenbach	after Winterhalter	I.B.
16.	Capriccio Espagnole	1939	Rimsky-Korsakov	Andreu	I.B.
17.	Mam'zelle Angot	Recreated			
		1947	Lecocq-Jacob	Derain	S.W.B.
18.	Donald of the Burthens	1951	Whyte	Colquhoun-MacBryde	S.W.B.

BALLETS BY NINETTE DE VALOIS

19.	Job	1931	Vaughan Williams	Piper	S.W.B.
20.	The Haunted Ballroom	1934	Toye	Motley	S.W.T.B.
21.	The Rake's Progress	1935	Gordon	Whistler	S.W.B., S.W.T.B.
22.	Checkmate	1937	Bliss	Kauffer	S.W.B.
23.	The Prospect Before Us	1940	Boyce	Furse	S.W.B., S.W.T.B.
24.	Don Quixote	1950	Gerhard	Burra	S.W.B.

BALLETS BY FREDERICK ASHTON

25.	Façade	1931	Walton	Armstrong	S.W.B., S.W.T.B.
26.	Les Rendezvous	1933	Auber	Chappell	S.W.T.B.
27.	Apparitions	1936	Liszt	Beaton	S.W.B.
28.	Nocturne	1936	Delius	Fedorovich	S.W.B.
29.	Les Patineurs	1937	Meyerbeer	Chappell	S.W.B.
30.	Wedding Bouquet	1937	Berners	Berners	S.W.B.
31.	Dante Sonata	1940	Liszt	Fedorovich	S.W.B.
32.	Symphonic Variations	1946	Franck	Fedorovich	S.W.B.
33.	Cinderella	1948	Prokofiev	Malclés	S.W.B.
34.	Scènes de Ballet	1948	Stravinsky	Beaurepaire	S.W.B.
35.	Dapnnis and Chloe	1951	Ravel	Craxton	S.W.B.
36.	Tiresias	1951	Lambert	Lambert	S.W.B.
37.	Sylvia	1952	Delibes	Ironside	S.W.B.

BALLETS BY GEORGES BALANCHINE

38.	Ballet Imperial	Tchaikovsky	Berman	S.W.B.

Twenty or more ballets by Balanchine could be added to this list, all of them important works, but opportunities of seeing them are rare. They are mostly in the repertoire of New York City Ballet: see them if you can.

BALLETS BY ANTHONY TUDOR

Tudor's ballets in the Ballet Rambert repertoire are all worth seeing. His later work has all been done in America and the only opportunity of seeing these ballets is when visiting American companies come to England.

BALLETS BY OTHER CHOREOGRAPHERS

The Ballet Rambert has long been a nursery for budding choreographers. In addition to Tudor's ballets the Ballet Rambert repertoire includes many excellent ballets including Andrée Howard's *Lady into Fox*, *The Sailor's Return* and *Death and the Maiden*, Walter Gore's *Simple Symphony* and several other works. Sadler's Wells Theatre Ballet repertoire includes Celia Francz's *Khadra*, and many ballets by John Cranko, notably *Sea Change*, *Beauty and the Beast*, *Harlequin in the Street*, and *Pineapple Poll*. *Bonne Bouche*, also by Cranko (music Oldham, décor Lancaster) is in the Sadler's Wells repertoire. Helpmann's ballets: *Adam Zero*, *Hamlet* and *Miracle in the Gorbals* have not been in the Sadler's Wells repertoire for several years, and there are no plans at present for reviving them: but if they are see them if you can.

In a Paris studio

I saw recently an advertisement of a recital to be given by a school of dancing. In one brief performance, it was announced, the pupils would perform " *Swan Lake, The Sleeping Beauty,* and other classics and solo dances." By all means let schools give performances for the pupils' mothers and aunts, but do not for one moment think that the recital can be called Ballet. Ballet, as I hope you will have learned in this book, is much, much more than just dancing a sequence of steps. In the same way do not think that you know all about ballet, after you have read this book. But if your interest has been aroused, and you would like to know more, then read some of the books mentioned on page 93, and read the magazines devoted to ballet: *The Dancing Times, Dance and Dancers, Ballet,* and *Ballet To-day,* and above all see as much ballet as you can, in the theatre and on television.